Easy Works for Windows® 95

Nat Gertler

Easy Works for Windows 95

Copyright © 1995 by Que® Corporation.

Library of Congress Catalog No: 95-71441

ISBN: 0-7897-0456-0

97 96 95   6 5 4 3 2 1

Interpretation of the printing code: the rightmost double-digit number is the year of the book's printing; the rightmost single-digit number, the number of the book's printing. For example, a printing code of 95-1 shows that the first printing of the book occurred in 1995.

Screen reproductions in this book were created with Collage Plus from Inner Media, Inc., Hollis, NH.

This book was produced digitally by Macmillan Computer Publishing and manufactured using 100% computer-to-plate technology (filmless process), by Shepard Poorman Communications Corporation, Indianapolis, Indiana.

Dedication

This book goes out to everyone who helps new users figure out how to use computers.

Next time you need someone's help, show them this dedication. Then tell them, "If you help me, that means this book will be dedicated to you!"

Credits

Publisher
Roland Elgey

Vice President and Publisher
Marie Butler-Knight

Editorial Services Director
Elizabeth Keaffaber

Publishing Manager
Barry Pruett

Managing Editor
Michael Cunningham

Development Editor
Ella Davis

Senior Production Editor
Michelle Shaw

Copy Editor
Audra Gable

Cover Designers
Dan Armstrong
Kim Scott

Designers
Barbara Kordesh
Amy Peppler-Adams

Indexer
Mary Jane Frisby

Production Team
Gary Adair, Claudia Bell,
Anne Dickerson, Damon Jordan,
Bob LaRoche, Mike Thomas,
Scott Tullis, Kelly Warner, Jody York

Illustration
Jason Hand, Clint Lahnen

Composed in *Stone Serif* and *MCPdigital* by Que Corporation

About the Author

Nat Gertler writes. He has written *Computers Illustrated* and *Multimedia Illustrated* for Que, as well as a lot of comic books. These include stories for "Jetsons," "ElfQuest," and "Blood Syndicate," and his own creations "Mister U.S." and "The Factor."

When he's not writing, Nat can be found at the video arcade or scouring flea markets for obscure "Peanuts" books. He eats far fewer donuts than some sections of this book may imply.

Acknowledgments

I'd like to thank the kind folks at Que who put up with my sometimes mis-aimed attempts to put as much into this book as possible. Large thanks go to Martha for signing me up for this, to Seta for keeping me rolling on it, and to Ella for catching me when I went astray. Thanks to Brad and Kathy-Jo for supporting my involvement. And an extra thank you to all those product development folks at Microsoft, without whom this book would be pretty pointless.

Trademark Acknowledgments

Contents

Easy Works for Windows 95

Part III: Using the Spreadsheet   96

Part IV: Using the Communications Program 148

Part V: Using the Database Program   168

Part VI: Using a TaskWizard 206

Part VII: Sample Documents 224

Part VIII: Reference Section 237

Index 245

Introduction

What You Can Do with Works

Microsoft Works for Windows 95 is a combination of a word processor, a spreadsheet program, a database program, and a communications program, all in one. The word processor turns your computer into a super typing tool. The spreadsheet program does many calculations quickly, which saves you time punching them into a calculator. The database program keeps track of lists of information and lets you change the list, sort it, and print out some or all of the items on it. The communications program enables you to use your computer to access the Internet and other communication services.

Specifically, you can use Works to:

- **Write.** You can write letters, reports, memos, or anything else you might type on a typewriter. With the word processor, you can check your spelling and change whatever you want before you print it out. And even after you print it, you can make changes and print it out again.

- **Reuse your writing.** Because you can save a copy of what you've written on your computer disk, you can reuse documents you've already written. You won't ever have to waste time retyping something you've already typed. And form letters don't look like form letters when you edit them on the computer.

- **Let someone else do the writing.** Works comes with dozens of letters already written for you. For example, if you need a thank you note, an apology, or a business proposal letter, you can start with one that was made up by experts and then change it as much as necessary to make it more personal. Works even includes suggestions on how to make the best use of these letters.

- **Design fancy pages.** Along with the word processor, you can use pictures and fancy lettering of different sizes to make your own stationery, party invitations, sales flyers, newsletters, or anything else that you want to look good.

■ **Calculate numbers.** If you want to create a budget, balance your checkbook, or figure your taxes, Works can do all the calculating for you. You type in all the numbers once and then tell Works what calculations to do. Works will add, subtract, multiply, divide, or do whatever fancy calculations you want it to. And if you change any of the numbers that you put in, Works automatically calculates everything again.

■ **Keep records of your calculations.** You can print your numbers and results so you can show it to other people or file it away. You can also store all your calculations on your hard disk so you can look at them again later. You can even store and print comments about what each number and calculation is so you'll be able to understand it later.

■ **Use pre-designed forms.** Works comes with sharp-looking forms already designed for you, including everything from customer order forms to student grade charts. The calculations are built into the forms, so when you enter the students' grades for each assignment, Works automatically calculates their grades for the term and the average for the whole class!

■ **Draw a graph.** Graphs are handy tools for business presentations. Works enables you to create and print out many types of graphs, including line graphs, bar graphs, and pie graphs.

■ **Keep a list.** You can use Works to keep track of your phone list, your customer list, your inventory, your record collection, or anything else that you keep a list of. Finding a single item in a long list is easy when you let the computer search for it.

■ **Print out a list.** You can print a hard copy of your list that you can carry around and show people. Even better, you can ask for just part of your list: you can get a list of just the clients who owe money, or just your Rolling Stones albums, or just your friends in California.

■ **Use computer services.** If your computer has a modem, you can exchange information with distant computers over telephone lines. You can get news, play games, send electronic mail, and get involved in conversations with people all over the world.

This book gives you a good start on using Works. Once you're comfortable with the basics of Works, you may want to read one of these books to become an advanced user:

The Complete Idiot's Guide to Works for Windows 95

Using Microsoft Works 95 Edition

Special Edition Using Microsoft Works for Windows 95

Task Sections

The Task sections include numbered steps that tell you how to accomplish certain tasks such as saving a workbook or filling a range. The numbered steps walk you through a specific example so that you can learn the task by doing it.

Big Screen

At the beginning of each task is a large screen that shows how the computer screen will look after you complete the procedure that follows in that task. Sometimes, the screen shows a feature discussed in that task, such as a shortcut menu.

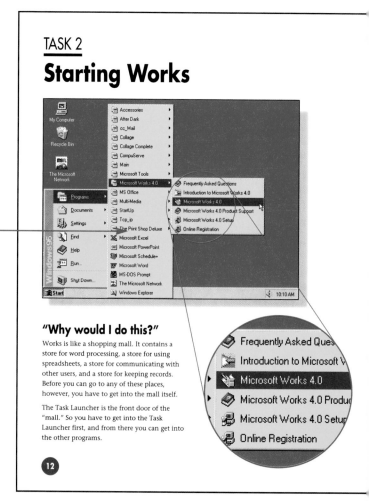

TASK 2

Starting Works

"Why would I do this?"

Works is like a shopping mall. It contains a store for word processing, a store for using spreadsheets, a store for communicating with other users, and a store for keeping records. Before you can go to any of these places, however, you have to get into the mall itself.

The Task Launcher is the front door of the "mall." So you have to get into the Task Launcher first, and from there you can get into the other programs.

12

Step-by-Step Screens

Each task includes a screen shot for each step
of a procedure that shows how the computer
screen will look at each step in the process.

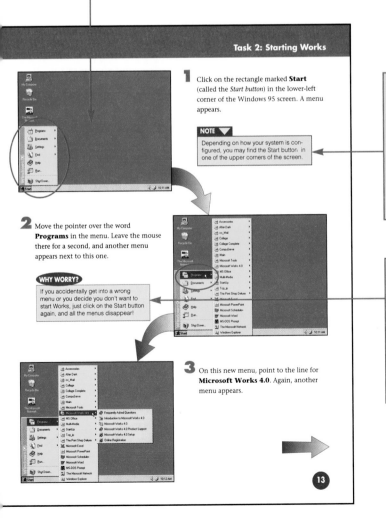

Task 2: Starting Works

1 Click on the rectangle marked **Start**
(called the *Start button*) in the lower-left
corner of the Windows 95 screen. A menu
appears.

NOTE
Depending on how your system is configured, you may find the Start button in
one of the upper corners of the screen.

Other Notes

Many tasks contain other short notes that tell
you a little more about certain procedures.
These notes define terms, explain other
options, refer you to other sections when
applicable, and so on.

2 Move the pointer over the word
Programs in the menu. Leave the mouse
there for a second, and another menu
appears next to this one.

WHY WORRY?
If you accidentally get into a wrong
menu or you decide you don't want to
start Works, just click on the Start button
again, and all the menus disappear!

Why Worry? Notes

You may find that you performed a task,
such as sorting data, that you didn't want to
do after all. The Why Worry notes tell you
how to undo certain procedures or get out of
a situation such as displaying a Help screen.

3 On this new menu, point to the line for
Microsoft Works 4.0. Again, another
menu appears.

13

PART I

Getting Started in Works

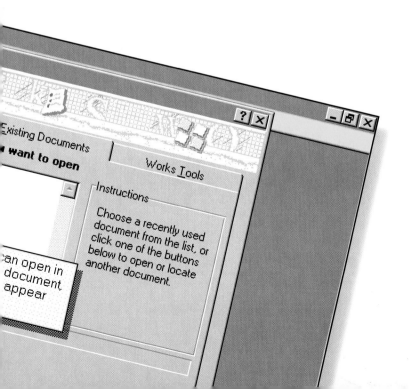

Works is made up of separate built-in programs that you use to do word processing, perform calculations, keep track of records, and communicate with other computers. These programs are designed to look and work similarly. Although the commands you use vary from program to program, the way that you give the commands is the same. So, once you learn how to use one of the programs, you are well on your way to being able to use all of them!

You don't even have to learn how to start each program in Works. Works has a single program called *Task Launcher* that exists just to help you start the other programs. Task Launcher can also help you find documents you've already saved on the hard disk.

In this Part, you learn how to start up the Task Launcher, as well as how to use the menus, command buttons, and other elements that appear in all Works programs. Many of these elements are also used in other Windows programs.

If you've used other Windows programs, you already know a lot of what's covered in this Part. You should still read through everything, though, because there are a number of tips that could help you use these elements better and more easily.

On the other hand, if you've never used Windows before, this Part will prove particularly helpful. Many of the things you learn here will work on almost any other Windows program you use. Learning to use Works will give you a running start on learning to use other programs.

This Part also teaches you how to use the Help commands, which enable you to ask the computer for help when you get stuck. Works has built-in answers to a lot of "How do I..." questions, and it has a system that's good at helping you find the answer you're looking for.

The similarity between programs and the available Help information make learning how to use Works easier than you probably expected. Don't let the long list of things that Works can do scare you. You don't have to learn everything at once; learn what you need to know now, and then, when you need to do something else, learn that!

After you've finished with this section, you'll probably want to read the next section, which teaches you how to use the word processor. Even if you don't think you're going to use the word processor, you might change your mind once you see how easy and useful it is. Some of the biggest fans of word processors are people who used to think they would never want to use them at all!

However, if you're not that interested in the word processor and want to jump ahead to other parts of the book, go ahead. If you want to learn to use Works to perform calculations, go to Part III, "Using the Spreadsheet." If you want to learn to use Works to access computer communications services, read Part IV, "Using the Communications Program." To get a handle on keeping lists, check out Part V, "Using the Database." Once you've read this Part, you will understand the tasks in any of those parts. In no time, you'll be using Works productively.

TASK 1
Using the Mouse

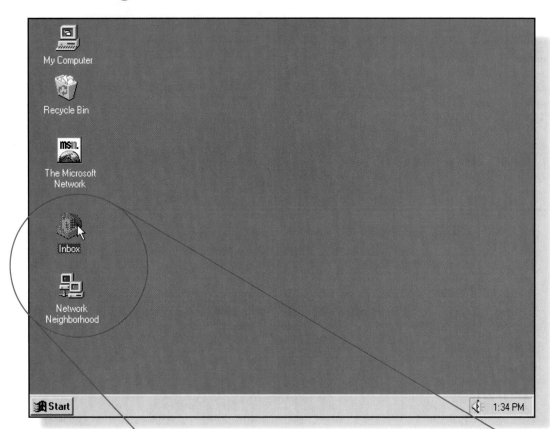

"Why would I do this?"

The mouse is a device you move around on your desk in order to move a pointer in a corresponding direction on the computer screen. You point to things on the screen and press the buttons on the mouse to tell the computer what you want it to do.

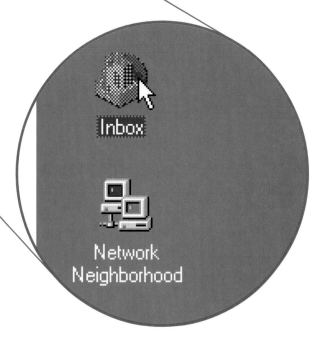

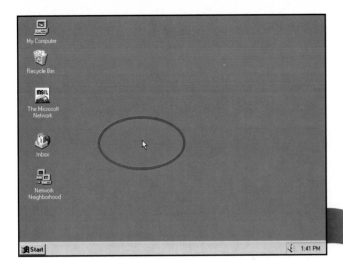

1 Push the mouse around on the desktop, and you see an arrow moving around the screen. If you move the mouse to the left, the arrow moves to the left. If you push the mouse forward, the arrow moves up. If you pull it back, the arrow moves down.

NOTE ▼

Sometimes the pointer turns into something besides an arrow. It turns into a picture of an hourglass when you have to wait for the computer to do something. When you're entering text, it becomes a large letter I.

2 You use the left mouse button to click and double-click. To *click* on something, position the mouse so that the pointer is over what you want to click on, and then tap the mouse button. The thing you click on usually changes (for example, the Inbox in this picture has turned blue). To *double-click*, point to an item and tap the mouse button twice quickly.

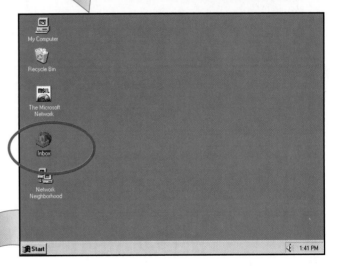

3 The right mouse button is not used very often. Usually, pressing the right mouse button causes a special menu to appear. ■

NOTE ▼

If you have a mouse with three buttons, you won't use the middle one while running Works.

Starting Works

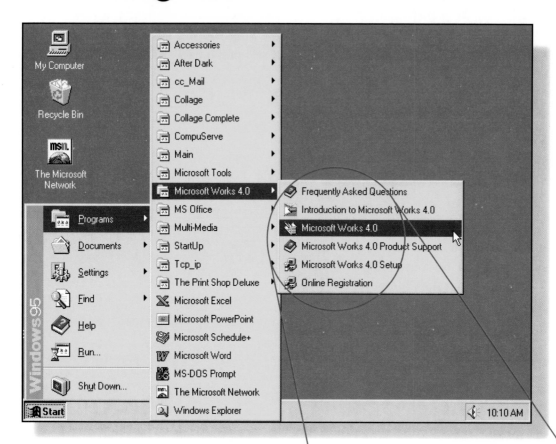

"Why would I do this?"

Works is like a shopping mall. It contains a store for word processing, a store for using spreadsheets, a store for communicating with other users, and a store for keeping records. Before you can go to any of these places, however, you have to get into the mall itself.

The Task Launcher is the front door of the "mall." So you have to get into the Task Launcher first, and from there you can get into the other programs.

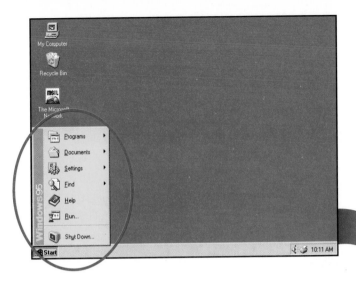

1 Click on the rectangle marked **Start** (called the *Start button*) in the lower-left corner of the Windows 95 screen. A menu appears.

NOTE ▼

Depending on how your system is configured, you may find the Start button in one of the upper corners of the screen.

2 Move the pointer over the word **Programs** in the menu. Leave the mouse there for a second, and another menu appears next to this one.

WHY WORRY?

If you accidentally get into a wrong menu or you decide you don't want to start Works, just click on the Start button again, and all the menus disappear!

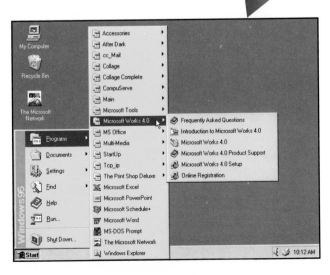

3 On this new menu, point to the line for **Microsoft Works 4.0**. Again, another menu appears.

4 The new menu also contains the choice of Microsoft Works 4.0. Click on it, and the program starts.

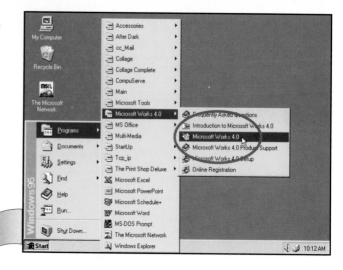

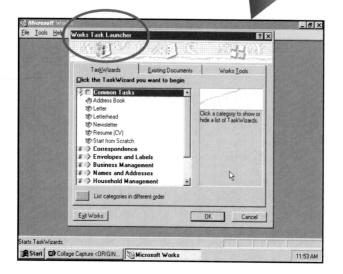

5 The Works Task Launcher screen appears, which lets you know that you have successfully started Works! ■

NOTE ▼

Your system might have a picture on the Windows screen labeled "Shortcut to Microsoft Works 4.0" (see the first figure). If it does, you can start Works more quickly by double-clicking (clicking twice) on it.

TASK 3

Using the Menus

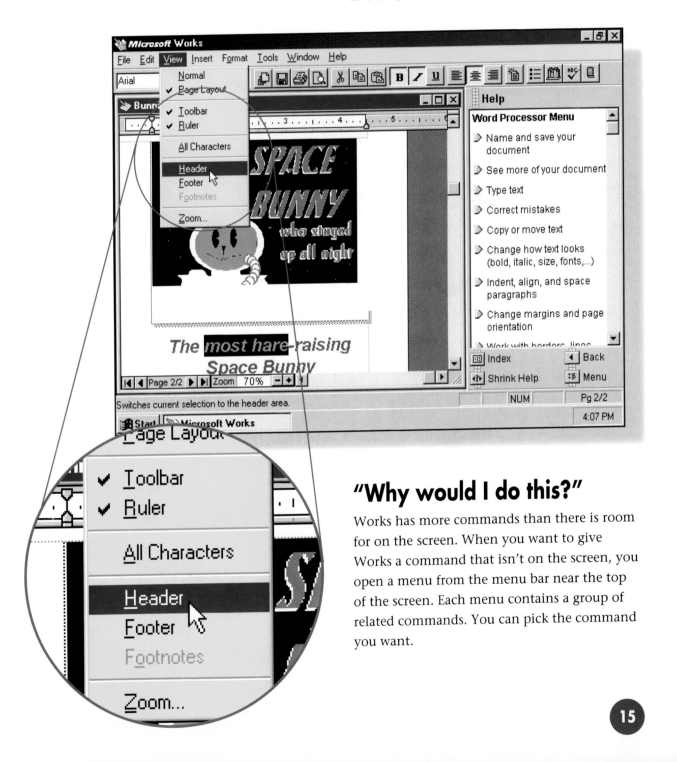

"Why would I do this?"

Works has more commands than there is room for on the screen. When you want to give Works a command that isn't on the screen, you open a menu from the menu bar near the top of the screen. Each menu contains a group of related commands. You can pick the command you want.

15

1 On the menu bar (the second bar from the top of the screen), click on the name of the menu you want to open. The name of the menu changes color, and a menu of commands appears below it.

WHY WORRY?

If you open the wrong menu or decide that you don't want to give a command, just click on the menu name again. The menu goes away!

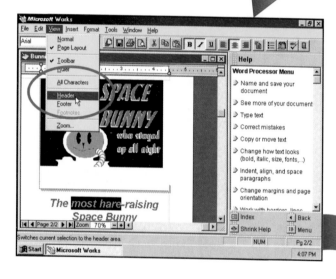

2 Click on the command you want to issue.

NOTE

You can select any command without using the mouse. To do so, press and hold the Alt key and press the letter that's underlined in the menu name, such as the F in "File." Then press the letter that's underlined in the command name.

3 Some commands (such as Save As...) have three dots after them. Those three dots (called an *ellipsis*) mean that if you choose that menu command, the computer will display a dialog box that asks you for more information. If a command is not followed by an ellipsis, the program carries out the command immediately. ■

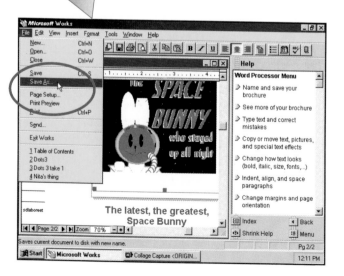

TASK 4
Using the On-Screen Buttons

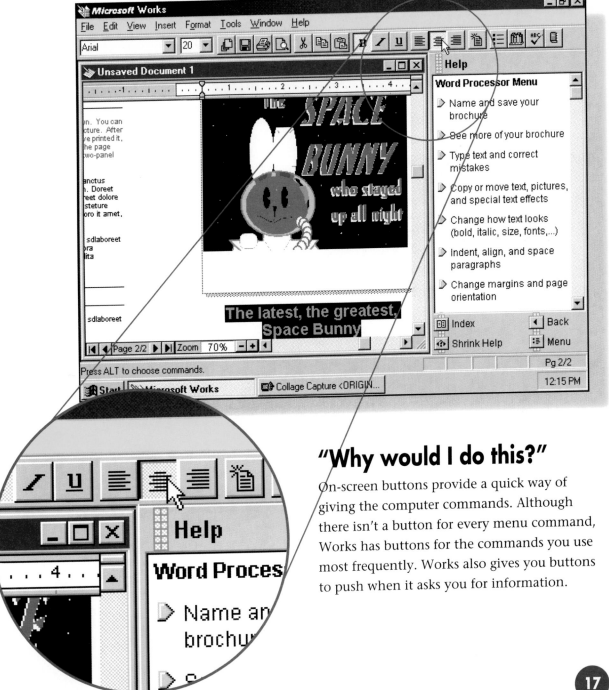

"Why would I do this?"

On-screen buttons provide a quick way of giving the computer commands. Although there isn't a button for every menu command, Works has buttons for the commands you use most frequently. Works also gives you buttons to push when it asks you for information.

1 To use a button, position the pointer over it and click on it. When you do, the button appears to be pushed in, and Works executes the command or displays a dialog box if necessary.

NOTE ▼

The row of buttons under the menu bar is called the *toolbar*.

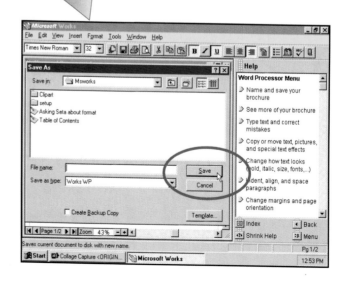

2 Some buttons bounce right back out after you use them, but some appear to stay pushed in. The ones that stay pushed in are like on/off switches for those commands. When the button is pushed, the corresponding feature is on; when the button is not pushed, the feature is turned off.

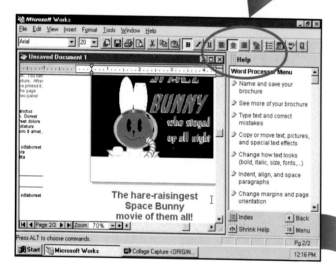

3 When Works asks for more information and gives you buttons, the buttons are a lot like menu selections. Each button has words on it describing what it does. ■

NOTE ▼

Some of these buttons have an underlined letter on them. You can press and hold Alt and press that letter instead of clicking on the button.

TASK 5
Using the Scroll Bars

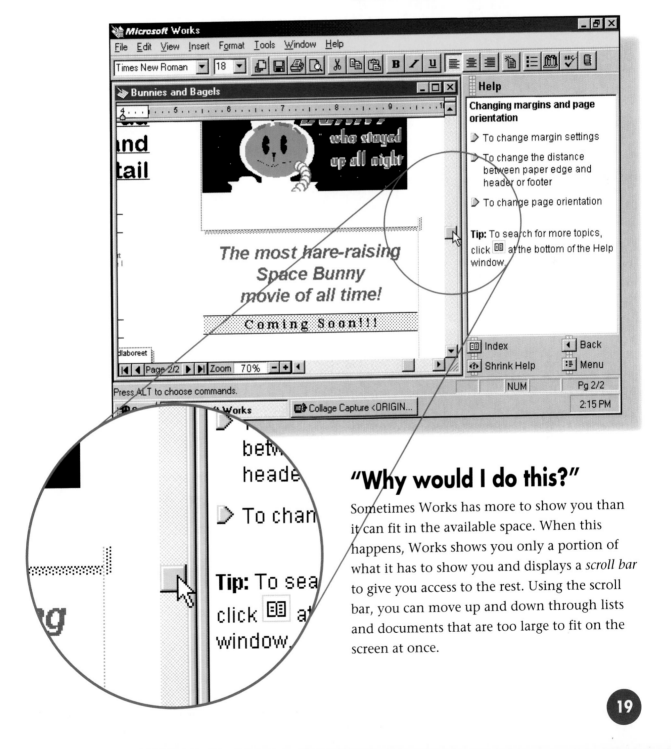

"Why would I do this?"

Sometimes Works has more to show you than it can fit in the available space. When this happens, Works shows you only a portion of what it has to show you and displays a *scroll bar* to give you access to the rest. Using the scroll bar, you can move up and down through lists and documents that are too large to fit on the screen at once.

1 The rectangle that appears to stand out from the scroll bar is called the *scroll box*; it shows you where you are in the document or list. If it's near the top of the bar, you're near the beginning of your document. If it's near the bottom of the bar, you're near the end of the document.

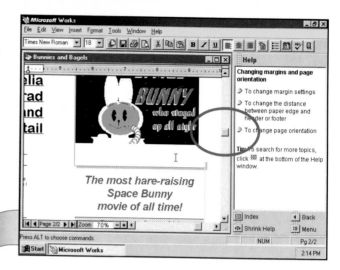

2 To move toward the beginning of your document, click on the up arrow button at the top of the scroll bar. This moves you up through the document a little at a time. Hold down the left mouse button to keep moving through the document until you reach the beginning.

3 To move toward the end of the document, click on the down arrow button at the bottom of the scroll bar. This moves you down through the document a little at a time. Hold down the left mouse button to keep moving through the document until you reach the end.

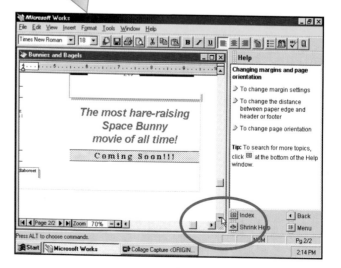

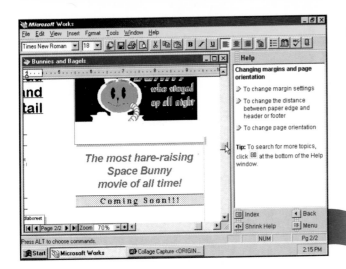

4 To go to a specific location in the document, place the mouse pointer on the scroll box, press and hold down the left mouse button, and drag the box to the approximate location you want. (Moving the mouse forward takes you toward the beginning of the document; moving it back takes you toward the end.)

5 When a document is too wide to fit in the available space, Works displays a horizontal scroll bar. You use this scroll bar to move left and right within the document just as you do the vertical scroll bar to move from top to bottom. ■

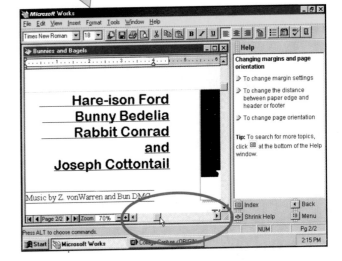

WHY WORRY?

Using the scroll bars doesn't change what's in your document, it only changes what part of the document you can see at the moment. You can always scroll back to what you were looking at before!

TASK 6

Getting Help with Task Launcher

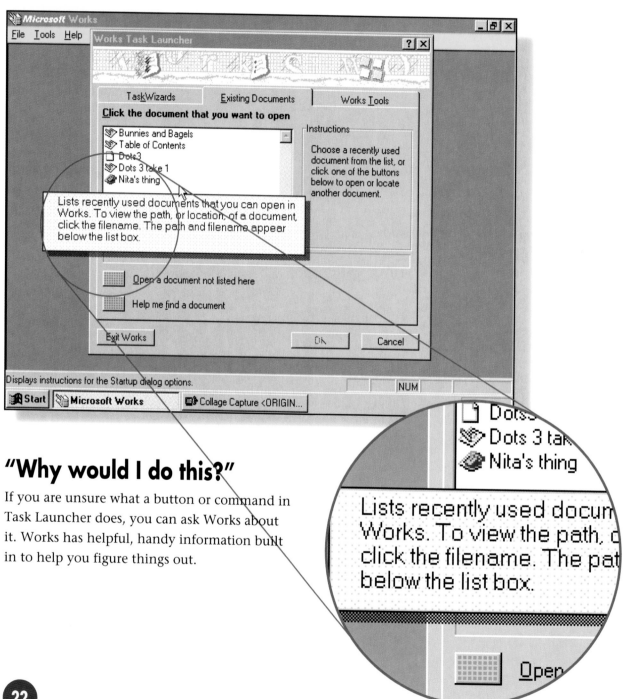

"Why would I do this?"

If you are unsure what a button or command in Task Launcher does, you can ask Works about it. Works has helpful, handy information built in to help you figure things out.

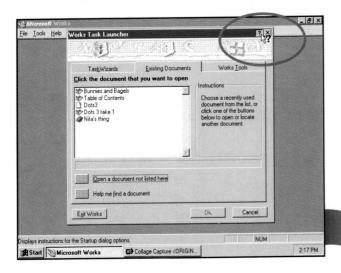

1 If you want to know how to use something in Task Launcher, click on the question mark button in the upper-right corner of the Task Launcher window. Your pointer becomes an arrow with a question mark next to it.

2 Click on the item about which you want more information, and Task Launcher displays a box containing an explanation of what that item does.

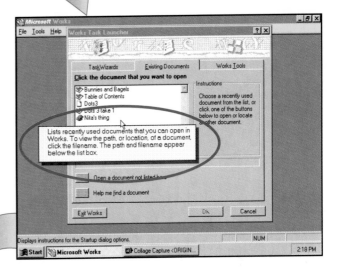

3 Continue with whatever you want to do. When you give the computer another command, the Help box disappears. ■

Getting Help with Other Parts of Works

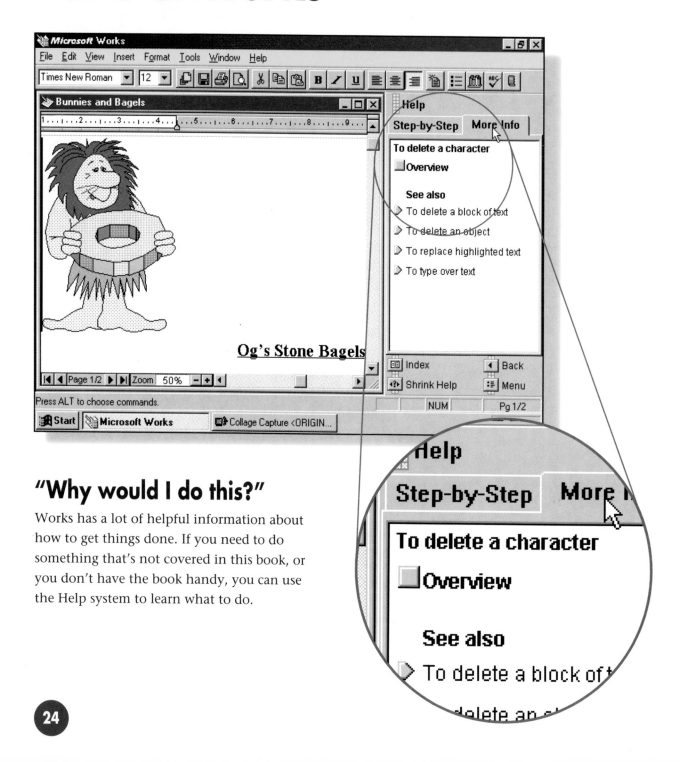

"Why would I do this?"

Works has a lot of helpful information about how to get things done. If you need to do something that's not covered in this book, or you don't have the book handy, you can use the Help system to learn what to do.

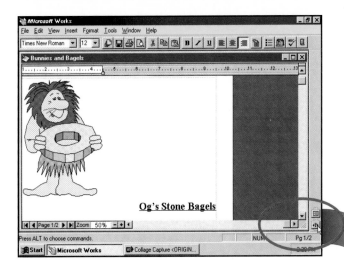

1 If there isn't a window with help information at the right side of the screen, click on the help button on the right edge of the screen. This opens the Help window, which contains information about the part of Works you are using.

2 Click on the button next to the item you want information on, and Works displays either another Help menu or step-by-step help on how to do what you want to do.

WHY WORRY?

If you select the wrong item from the Help menu, click the Back button to go back to the previous menu.

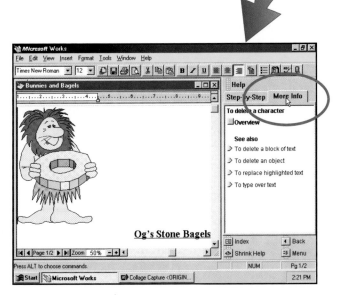

3 If you get to the step-by-step instructions and they aren't what you were looking for, click on the **More Info** button. This accesses another Help menu with more possibilities.

4 If you don't quite find what you are looking for in the menus, click on the **Index** button. Works displays an index of Help topics.

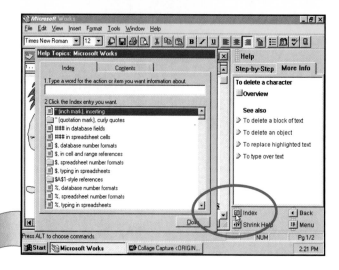

5 Type the topic you are looking for. Works displays an alphabetical list of Help topics, starting with the one you typed.

> **NOTE** ▼
>
> If the index doesn't have anything on the topic you requested, try typing in another name for the same thing.

6 When you find the topic you are looking for in the index, click on it. The Help information shows up in the Help box at the right or in a separate window.

> **NOTE** ▼
>
> If the item has a picture of a folder next to it in the Index entry list, clicking on it will display another list of Help topics. Click on the one you want.

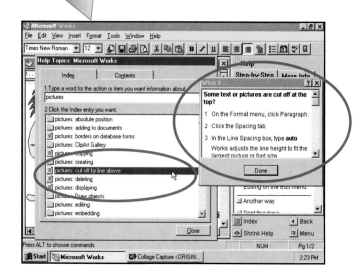

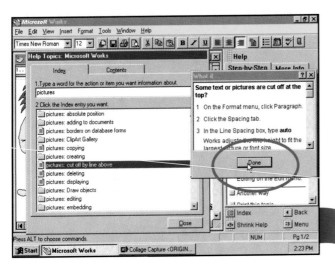

7 When you're done with a Help window, click on the **Done** button, and the window disappears.

8 When you're done with the index, click on the **Close** button, and the index disappears.

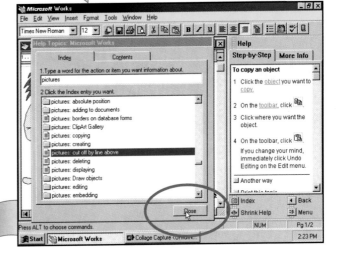

9 If you don't need help at this point and want more room on the screen for your documents, click on the **Shrink Help** button. Works eliminates the Help area and leaves just the Help and Index icons along the right edge of the screen. ■

TASK 8
Leaving the Task Launcher

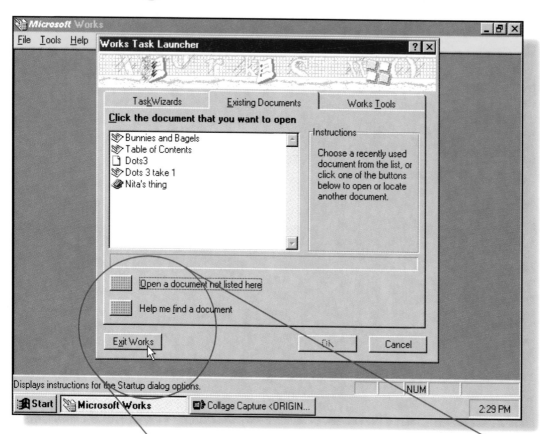

"Why would I do this?"

When you finish with your work (for at least a while), you can leave Task Launcher. When you do, it closes the Works program altogether, leaving your computer free so you can run other programs or turn it off.

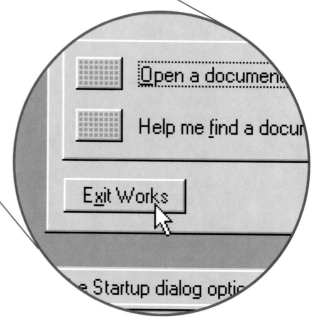

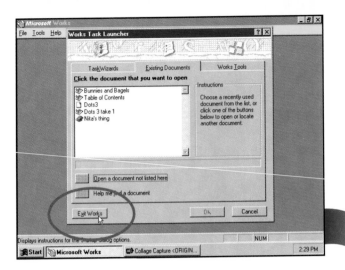

1 Click on the **Exit Works** button at the bottom of the Task Launcher screen.

2 When you leave Works, you are returned to the Windows 95 desktop. ∎

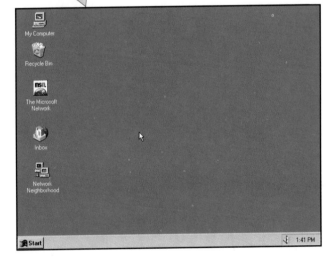

Spacebun

Once upon a time, a long, long time from now, there were (or will be) three space bunnies: Momma Space Bunny, Papa Space Bunny, and Hubert Horatio Frankandbeans Space Bunny. Papa Space Bunny was big, kindly, and had a nice singing voice. Mama Space Bunny was bigger, just as kind, and knew an awful lot about the O'Sullivan Nebula, where she was born. Hubert Horatio Bunny was a little boy bunny with a lot of energy and a huge imagination.

Mama and Papa Space Bunny used to joke about how big Hubert's imagination was. "That boy's got an imagination twice as big as McGee's Star," Mama would say. Hubert would look out of the porthole of the spaceship where they lived. He'd look into the sky at McGee's star and say "that's not very big at all!" He'd put his paws very close together and say "I can see it, and it's only this big!"

Pg 1/1

4:02 PM

Microsoft Works

File Edit View Insert Format Tools Window Help

Times New Roman 12 **B** *I* <u>U</u>

Spacebun

Header

Once upon a time

Page 1/1   Zoom 100%

T to choose commands.

Microsoft Works

Microsoft Works

File Edit View Insert Format Tools Window Help

Times New Roman 12 **B** *I* <u>U</u>

Bunnies and Bagels

Header

Zoom 50%

3 1/2   commands.

Help

Word Processor Menu

- Name and save your document
- See more
- Type
- C

Microsoft Works

File Edit View Insert Format Tools

Times New Roman 12

Unsaved Document 1

Header

Page 1/1

Bunnies and Bagels

The most har
Space Bu

Pg 1/2

7:02 PM

PART II

Using the Word Processor

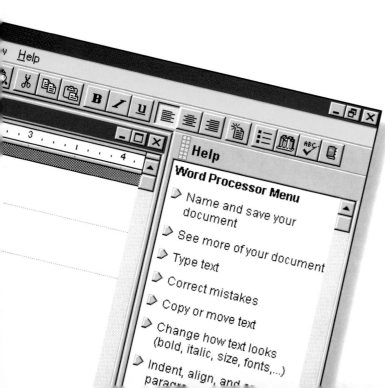

31

Bold

Italic

<u>Underline</u>

The word processor in Works enables you to use your computer as a very fancy typewriter. You can use it to write letters, stories, and reports and even to make up fancy brochures. You type everything into the computer, and it shows up on the screen. Then you can correct mistakes and rearrange the text in your document until it's just the way you want it. When you're happy with your document, you print it out.

You can also store the document on your computer's hard disk so you can refer to it later, make more changes, or even use pieces of this document to create another document. If you write a particular type of letter frequently (such as a late payment notice or a letter thanking Grandma for the socks she sent you), you only have to write it once. From then on, you can reuse the same letter and change only the important details (the name and address of the person who is late on his payments, or the color of the socks), and print it again! (Of course, Grandma might catch on after a while.)

The word processor enables you to do many things you can't do with a typewriter. You can easily format your text, you can put pictures in your documents, and you can choose different type styles to make your document look serious or humorous or friendly.

Works can even help you write your document! It has prewritten letters available for everything from a business solicitation to a personal apology. You pick the letter you want, and Works helps you change it so it looks like you made it (and not like a form letter). To get to these pre-written letters, you use a special Works tool called a Task Wizard. Because Task Wizards can also be used with the spreadsheet and database programs, they are not discussed in this section. Part VI gives you a full explanation on how to use Task Wizards.

Most of the word processor screen looks like a big white sheet of paper where you type. The rest of the screen is filled with menus and buttons that you use to control the way your document looks. You may never use some of these commands, but you will use others constantly. It's not important to know how everything works right from the start because there's a lot you won't be using. However, it won't hurt to learn a new command from time to time; you never know when you might find a feature or command that will help you do more work with less effort.

In this section, you will learn a number of ways to position your words just where you want them on the page. One task shows you how to center words across the page. Other tasks show how to give your paragraphs a smooth left edge, a smooth right edge, or both. You will also see how to adjust your margins to increase or decrease the amount of white space at the edge of the page and how to use the Tab key to line up information.

Once you've learned to use these, you might want to investigate other ways you can control the position of text. With the help of the Help system, study such features as the following:

■ *Indents*, which let you move the sides of the text further in from the edge of the paper.

■ *Subscripts* and *superscripts*, which put text slightly above or below the rest of the text on the line (footnotes, for example).

■ *Columns*, which will make your newsletter look more like a newspaper!

Works also has a lot of ways to make your words stand out more. The tasks in this section show you how to use different type styles and make your letters thicker, slanted, underlined, bigger, or smaller. Once you're comfortable using these features, try learning to use:

■ *Colors* to make certain words show up (this only works if you have a color printer).

■ *Borders* and *shading* to put words in a box or give them some background color.

■ *WordArt*, which is a bit complicated to use, but lets you design your own logos using outlined curved letters with shadows under them and other fancy things!

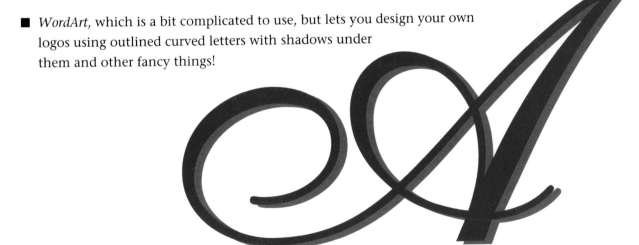

TASK 9
Starting a New Document

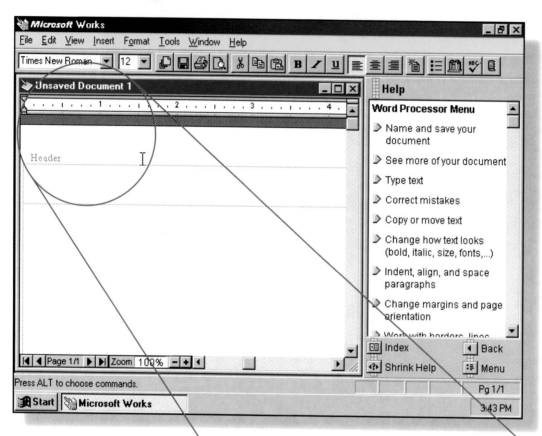

"Why would I do this?"

Starting a new document in the word processor is like sitting down at a typewriter and inserting a blank piece of paper. When you give the command to start a new document, your word processor displays a blank document, ready for you to start typing.

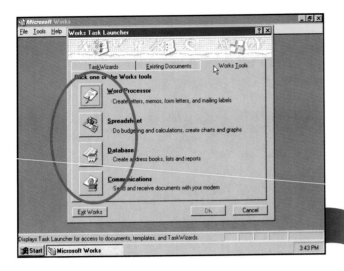

1 On the Task Launcher screen, click the **Works Tools** tab. The Works Tools tab contains four buttons, one for each of the main programs in Works.

2 Click the **Word Processor** button.

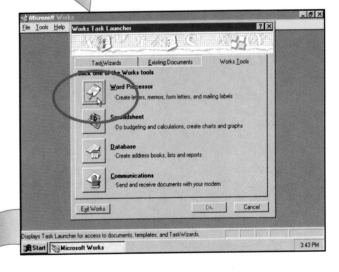

3 The word processor screen appears, with a blank document that you can type in. The white area of the screen represents your document. The rest of the screen contains tools you can use to edit the document. ■

NOTE ▼

The document has some gray lines and the word **Header** on it. These are guidelines that show you where things go; they won't appear on the document when you print it out. If you don't want to see them, pull down the View menu and select Normal.

35

Opening a Document You've Already Started

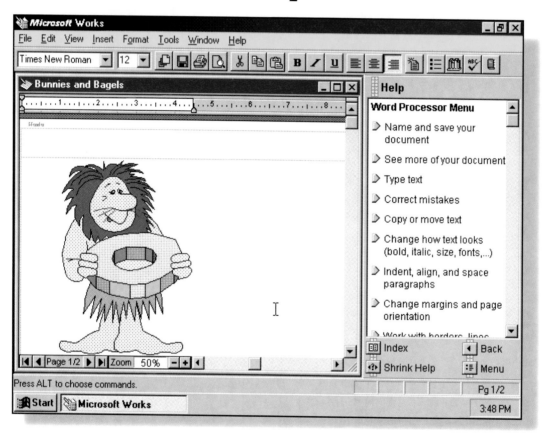

"Why would I do this?"

When you use the Works word processor, you will probably save your writing on your computer's disk. If you do, you can start writing a letter one day and finish it days (or weeks) later; you can check your old letters to see what you wrote in them; and you can even retrieve a letter you wrote to one person, change it around a bit, and send it to someone else!

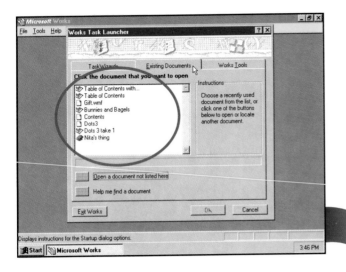

1 On the Task Launcher screen, click the **Existing Documents** button. This will bring up a list of documents you've worked with recently.

2 In that list, double-click on the name of the document you are looking for. (The word processor documents have a picture of a pencil and paper next to their names.) Works gets the document, starts the word processor, and displays the document in the word processor screen, ready for you to edit.

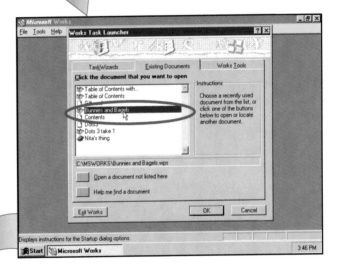

3 If your document is not in that list, click the **Open a document not listed here** button.

4 Works displays the Open dialog box, which contains a more complete list of documents. If your document appears in the list, double-click on it.

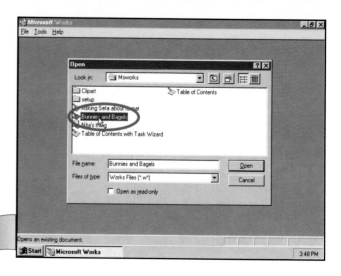

5 If you stored the document in one of the listed folders, double-click on that folder name, and the list changes to display the documents in that folder. Double-click on the name of your document.

NOTE ▼

The box labeled "Look in" tells you which folder's contents are listed. If you want to look in a different folder, click the button with the picture of a folder with an arrow on it. This brings you up out of that folder.

6 The document you chose appears on-screen, ready for you to edit. ■

WHY WORRY?

If you retrieve the wrong document, pull down the File menu and select the Close command to close it without saving it. This doesn't mess up the document you retrieved, and you can go back to the Task Launcher to get the right one!

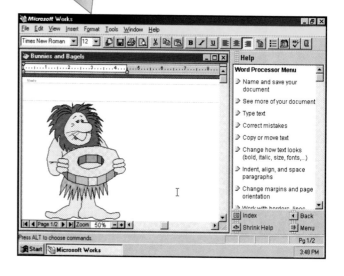

Typing

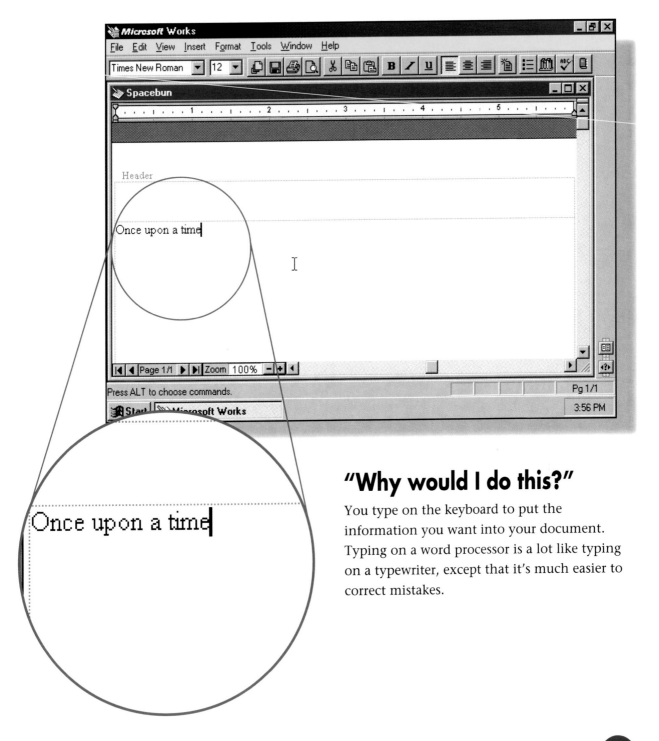

"Why would I do this?"

You type on the keyboard to put the information you want into your document. Typing on a word processor is a lot like typing on a typewriter, except that it's much easier to correct mistakes.

1 The blinking vertical line on the screen is called the *cursor* or *insertion point*. When you type, the character you type appears where the cursor was, and the cursor moves ahead to where the next character will appear.

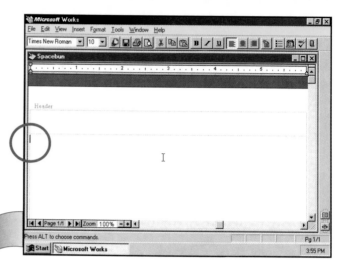

2 The basic process of typing on a computer keyboard is just like that of typing on a typewriter. Press a letter key, and that letter appears on the screen. To type a capital letter, hold down the **Shift** key and press the letter key.

> **NOTE** ▼
>
> If you hold down a character key, the computer reacts as if you were hitting that key repeatedly. It prints the letter to your screen continuously until you take your finger off.

3 One difference between typing on a word processor and on a standard typewriter is that you don't have to end each line before you get to the margin. The computer knows when you reach the margin, and it automatically wraps your text to the next line, taking care not to break words in the middle.

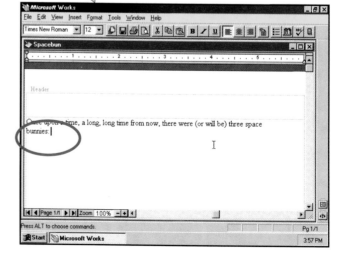

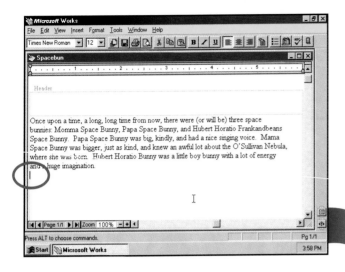

4 When you want to start a new line (for example, if you are starting a new paragraph), press the **Enter** key. This moves you to the start of the next line.

5 To indent a new line, press the **Tab** key. To indent further, hit that key again.

> **NOTE** ▼
>
> The Tab key always indents the same distance from the beginning of a new line so the lines you indent align properly.

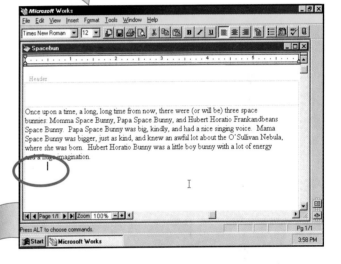

6 If you accidentally type the wrong letter, or you hit Tab or Enter when you don't mean to, just press the **Backspace** key to erase it. (This key may be labeled with an arrow pointing left, with the word Backspace, or with "bkspc.") ■

Moving the Cursor

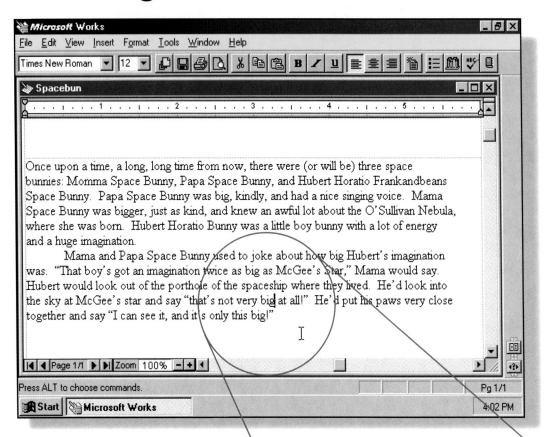

"Why would I do this?"

The cursor indicates where the text you type will appear. You can change and add things at the beginning, the middle, or the end of your document by moving the cursor to the desired location.

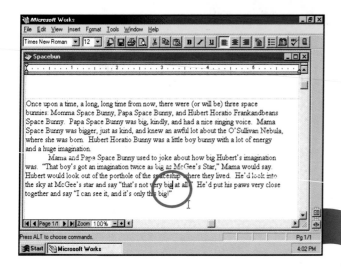

1 The four arrow keys grouped together on your keyboard are called the *cursor movement keys*. Press the up cursor key to move the cursor up one line. Press the down cursor key to move it down one line. Press the left and right cursor keys to move the cursor to the left or right.

2 Press the **Home** key to move the cursor to the beginning of the line it is currently on.

> **NOTE** ▼
>
> If your keyboard has a set of cursor movement keys mixed in with a set of number keys, you need to make sure **Num** Lock is turned off (that's the feature that makes these keys function as number keys instead of cursor keys). If you see **NUM** on your screen below and to the right of the document, hit the Num Lock key. The **NUM** sign disappears, and these keys work as cursor keys.

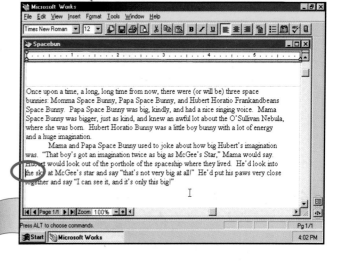

3 Press the **End** key to move the cursor to the end of the line it is currently on.

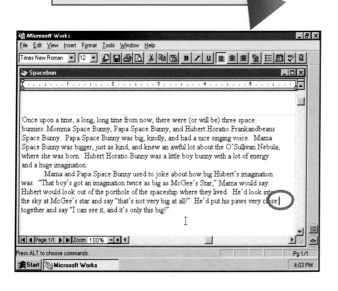

4 Press the **PgDn** key, and the cursor leaps ahead by half as much as the word processor can display in one screen. It also changes the display to show the part of the document to which the cursor moves.

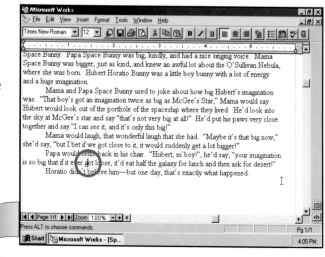

5 Press the **PgUp** key, and the cursor leaps back by half as much as the word processor can display in one screen. It also changes the display to show the part of the document to which the cursor moves.

6 To be able to type in an exact spot on the screen, move your mouse. Place the I-shaped pointer so that the bar of the I is to the right of the character you want to start typing after. Click the mouse button, and the cursor appears there. ■

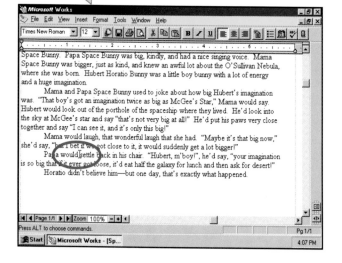

Zooming In and Out

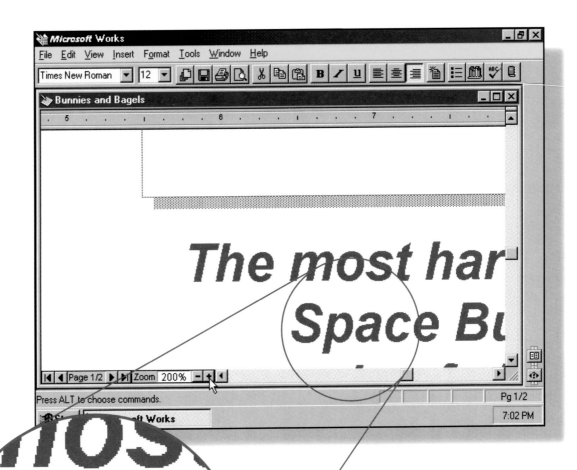

"Why would I do this?"

Sometimes you'll want to see as much of your document as possible on the screen. Other times, you'll want to get the closest possible look at a small part of your document, which makes it easier to find mistakes. The zoom control works a lot like a zoom lens on a camera: you can adjust it to get a close-up look at something small, a wide look at something larger, or something in between.

1 To fit more of the document on your screen, click the **Zoom Minus** button, and Works shrinks the display of your document. The zoom readout shows you how big it is compared to normal size; the smallest is 50%, or half normal size.

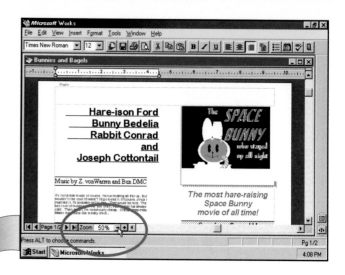

2 To get a close-up look at part of your document, click the **Zoom Plus** button. Again, the zoom readout shows you how big it is compared to normal size; the largest is 400%, which is four times normal size.

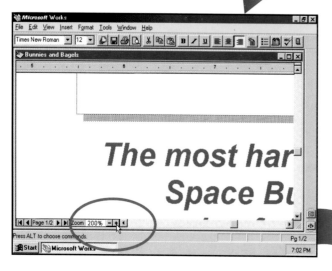

3 When you take a close-up look, you may need to use the scroll bars to view the part of the document you really want to see. ■

WHY WORRY?

Zooming in and out doesn't change what the document looks like when you print it, just how it appears on the screen!

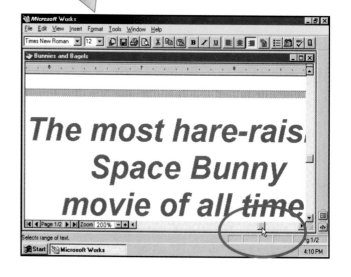

Selecting Text

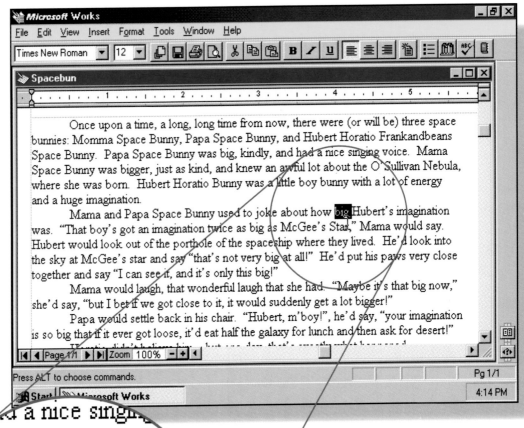

"Why would I do this?"

To copy, move, or change the look of just some of your text, you must indicate which part of your document you want to work with. You select text to indicate a smaller part of the document.

1 Position your cursor just before the first letter of the text you want to select.

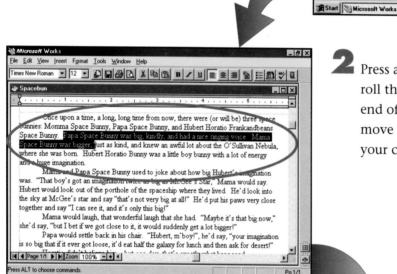

2 Press and hold the left mouse button and roll the mouse until the pointer is at the end of the text you want to select. As you move the mouse, a black box moves with your cursor.

3 Release the mouse button, and the text appears highlighted (white text on a black background).

> **NOTE** ▼
>
> Once you select more than one word, you have to select whole words only (even if you started or ended your selection with the cursor in the middle of a word).

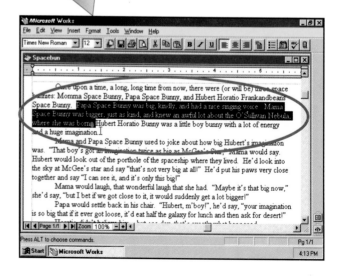

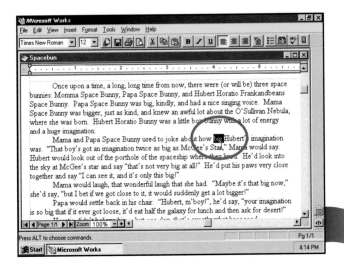

4 To select a single word, double-click on it.

5 To select a whole line, click to the left of the gray margin line and even with the desired line of text. Works highlights the whole line.

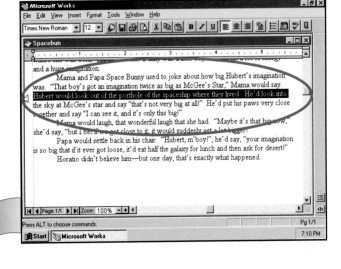

NOTE ▼

If you double-click to the left of the gray margin line, Works highlights the whole paragraph.

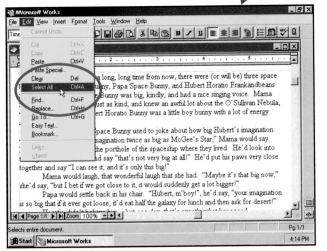

6 To select the whole document, pull down the **Edit** menu and choose **Select All**. ■

WHY WORRY?

Don't worry if you select the wrong part of your document. Selecting does not change your document, it's just the step you take before you make changes. To fix the problem, click anywhere in your document, and what you selected isn't selected anymore!

TASK 15
Erasing Text

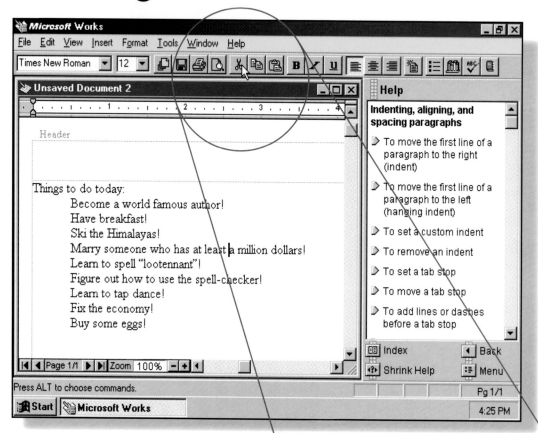

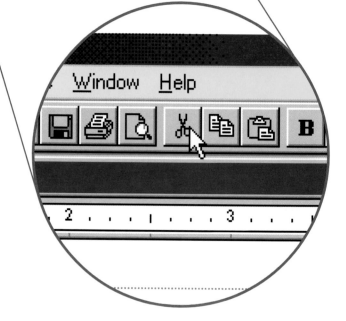

"Why would I do this?"

When you decide you don't like something you typed in your document, you can erase it. This is the same as crossing out something you type on a typewriter or erasing something written in pencil. But when you do it with a word processor, no one can tell you've erased anything!

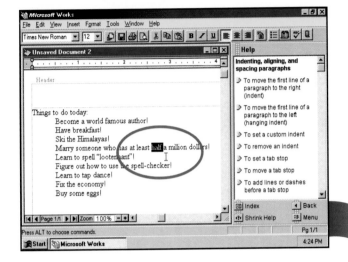

1 Select the text you want to erase.

2 Click the **Cut** button on the toolbar. The selected text disappears, and the text after the erased text moves over to fill the space. ■

WHY WORRY?

If you accidentally erase the wrong text, just open the Edit menu and select the Undo Editing command. The text reappears!

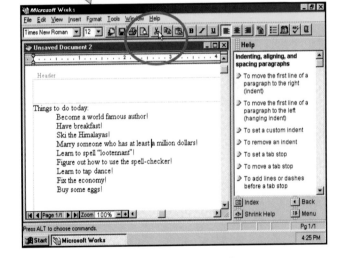

TASK 16
Moving Text

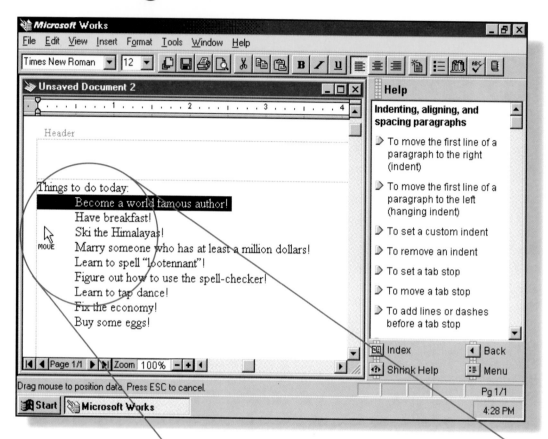

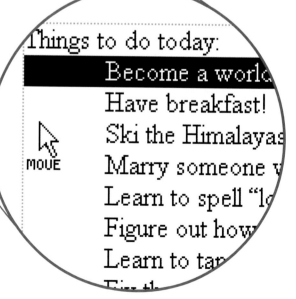

"Why would I do this?"

Sometimes when you reread a document, you find that although you said what you wanted to say, you didn't organize your ideas well. For example, you might realize that it is wiser to tell your grandma that you secretly got married last year before you tell her you're about to have a baby, instead of the other way around. By moving text, you can rearrange things in your document without having to delete them from one place and retype them in another!

52

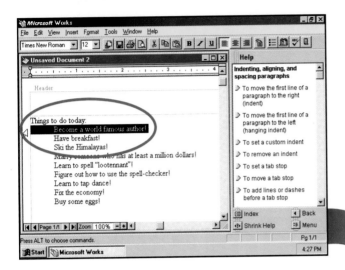

1 Select the text that you want to move.

2 Position the pointer over the selected text, and the pointer turns into an arrow with the word DRAG underneath it.

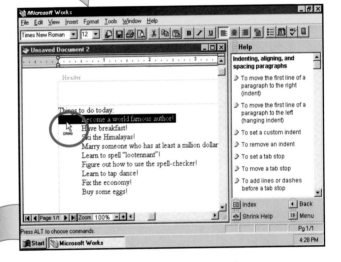

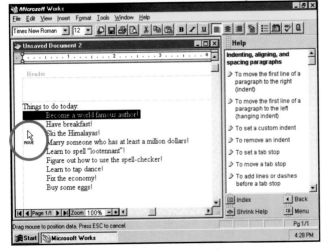

3 Press and hold the left mouse button, and move the pointer. The cursor follows the pointer, and the word under the arrow changes to MOVE.

NOTE ▼

The cursor won't follow the pointer beyond the end of a line of text.

4 Position the pointer in the location where you want to move the text.

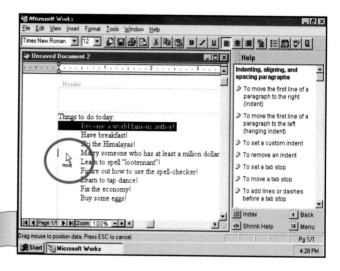

5 Release the mouse button. The text disappears from its original location and appears in the new location. ■

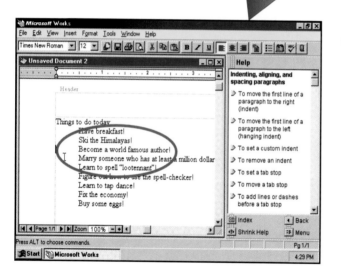

WHY WORRY?

If you accidentally select the wrong text to move, or you move it to the wrong place, just open the Edit menu and select the Undo Drag and Drop command. Works puts that text right back where it was originally!

TASK 17

Copying Text

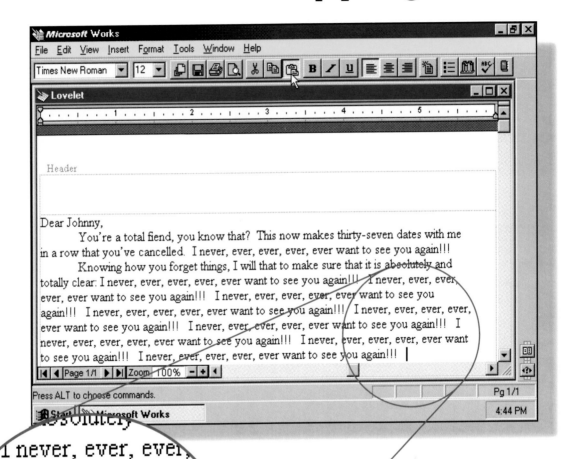

"Why would I do this?"

If you want to repeat something you've already typed in a document, you can save time by copying it instead of retyping it. Even if you want something that's a little different from what you have already typed, it can be faster to copy what you have typed, and then change the copy as necessary.

55

1 Select the text you want to copy.

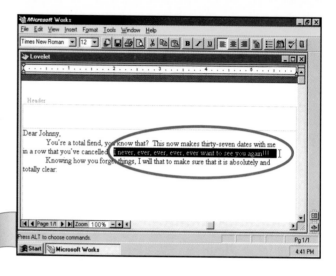

2 Click the **Copy** button on the toolbar.

3 Click on the location where you want to place the copied text. The blinking cursor appears there.

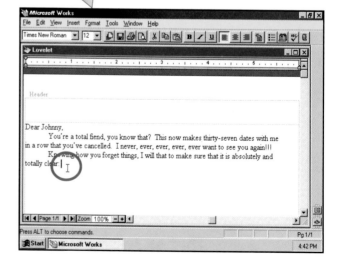

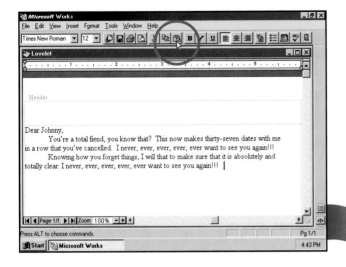

4 Click the **Paste** button. Works places the copied text in the cursor location.

WHY WORRY?

If you paste the wrong text, or put it in the wrong place, just open the Edit menu and select the Undo Editing command. The copy that you just pasted is gone!

5 If you want to make several copies of the same text, repeat steps 3 and 4 as many times as you want. ■

NOTE ▼

The text on the Clipboard stays there until you copy, cut, or move another block of text. You can click the Paste button at any time to place the Clipboard's contents in your document.

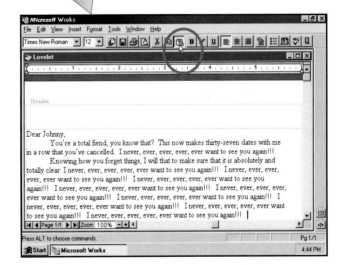

Making Text Bold, Italic, or Underlined

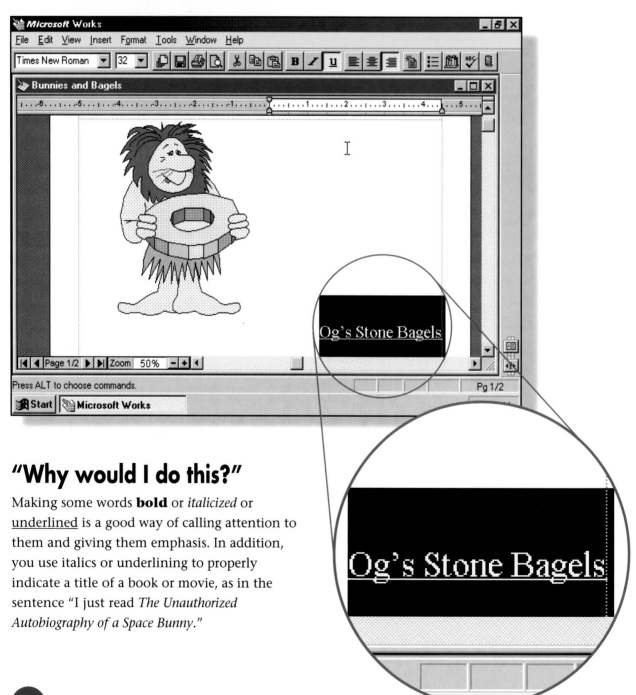

"Why would I do this?"

Making some words **bold** or *italicized* or <u>underlined</u> is a good way of calling attention to them and giving them emphasis. In addition, you use italics or underlining to properly indicate a title of a book or movie, as in the sentence "I just read *The Unauthorized Autobiography of a Space Bunny*."

1 Select the text you want to make bold, italic, or underlined.

NOTE ▼

When you click on the Bold, Italic, or Underline button and no text is selected, you're telling Works to turn on the feature. As a result, everything you type will have that style until you click the button again.

2 Click the toolbar button for the change you want to make: the button with a **B** for bold, the one with an **I** for italics, or the one with a **U** for underline.

NOTE ▼

Instead of clicking the button, you can hold down the Ctrl key and press B for bold, I for italics, or U for underline.

3 Works displays the text with the selected formatting. Note that the text is still selected; click anywhere else in the document to remove the highlight. ∎

WHY WORRY?

If you bold, italicize, or underline text and you don't like it, just select the text again. The button should look pushed in. Click that button, and Works returns the text to normal!

Changing the Font

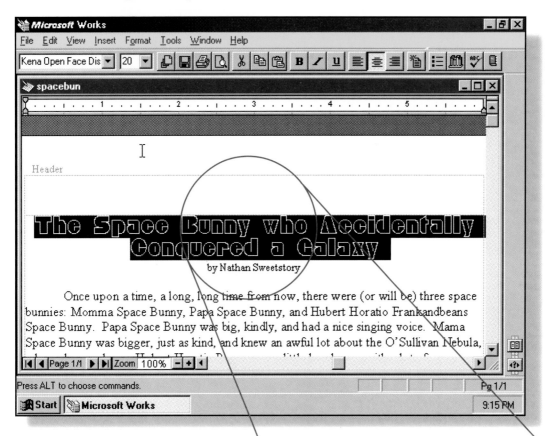

"Why would I do this?"

The *font* is the design of the letters, numbers, and other characters that make up your document. You can change the style and the design of the characters to make your writing look friendlier or more businesslike, or to create a simple logo for yourself. By changing the size, you can create headlines that stand out, or you can make everything so big that your Uncle Abdul, whose eyesight isn't so good anymore, can read the letters you write him.

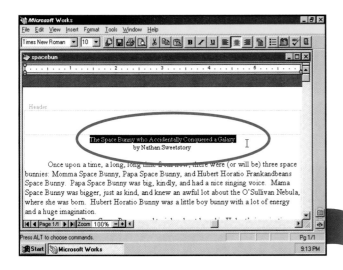

1 Select the text you want to change.

2 Click the down arrow button next to the font style box at the far left end of the toolbar. Works displays a list of available fonts. As you look through the list, you see that each font name appears in its own style so you can tell what the style looks like.

NOTE

Some of the style names in the list won't be readable. This can mean a number of things: the style is hard to read in small sizes; the style only has capital letters; or the style is a special symbol font and is no good for regular text.

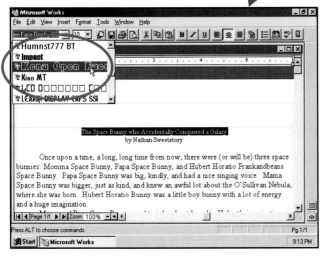

3 Scroll through the list to find a style you like. When you decide on a style, click on it.

61

4 The selected text takes on the selected style, and the name of that style appears in the style box.

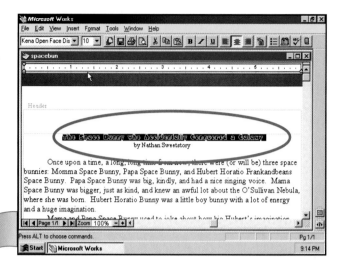

5 Click the down arrow button next to the font size display on the toolbar. In the list of sizes that appears, click on the one you want.

NOTE ▼

Fonts are measured in points, and the size refers to how many points high the line of type is. There are 72 *points* in an inch. The most commonly used sizes are 10 points and 12 points.

6 The selected text changes to the size you picked, and that size appears in the font size display. The text remains selected; to remove the highlight, click anywhere outside of the selected area. ■

WHY WORRY?

If you don't like the font or size you picked, just go back and pick another one!

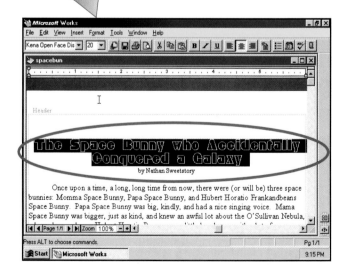

TASK 20

Moving Text Toward the Center or the Right Edge

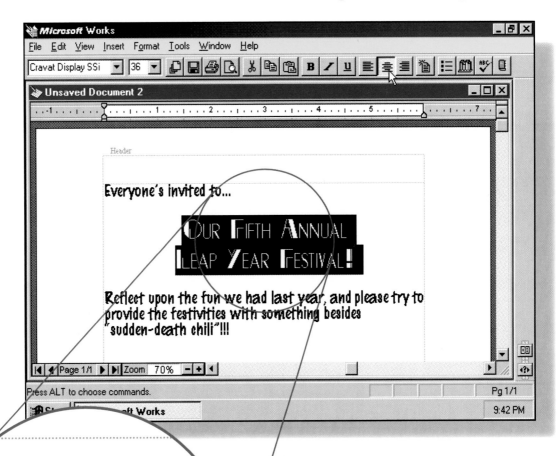

"Why would I do this?"

Unless you tell it otherwise, Works assumes that you want each line of text to start right up against the left margin. However, if you prefer, you can tell it to center the line horizontally on the page, which is good for titles or for a decorative touch. You can also tell it to move the text to the right so the end of each line is against the right margin, which is useful when you want a date in the upper-right corner of the page.

63

1 To move text you've already typed, first select the text.

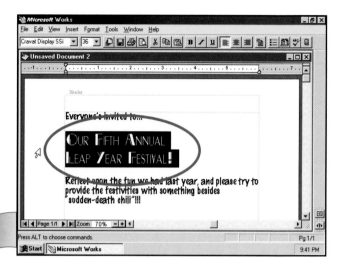

2 To center the text, click the **Center Align** button. The button appears to be pressed in, and Works centers the text on the page.

> **NOTE** ▼
>
> If you add text to a section you have already centered, Works centers it automatically.

3 To move the text to the right margin, click the **Right Align** button. The button appears to stick in, and Works aligns the text smoothly against the right margin. (It is uneven along the left side.)

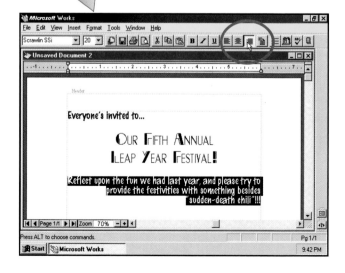

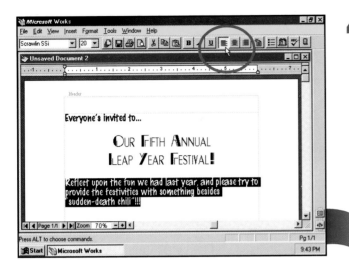

4 To get the text back to normal, push the **Left Align** button, which aligns the text smoothly against the left margin. (It is uneven along the right side.)

NOTE ▼

Text aligned with the left margin is by far the easiest to read. Centered and right-aligned text is okay for short sections, but you shouldn't align a whole letter or story that way.

5 If you click one of the alignment buttons when no text is selected, everything you type from that point on is aligned accordingly, until you pick another alignment or move the cursor elsewhere. ■

WHY WORRY?

If you don't like the current alignment of your text, just select the text and pick the alignment button you want!

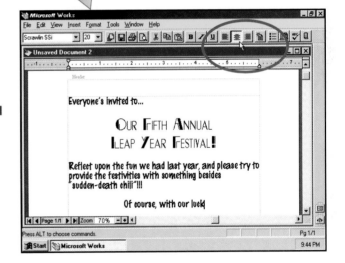

Making Text Even on Both Sides

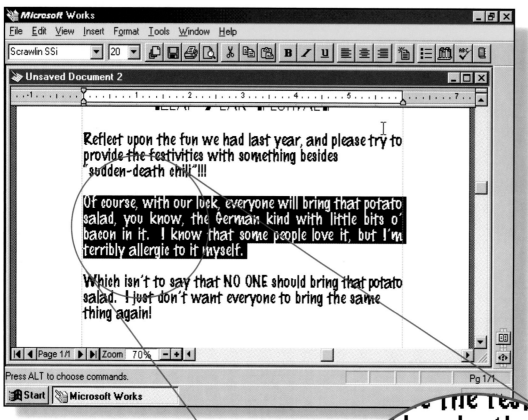

"Why would I do this?"

Text that is even down both sides of the page has a very professional squared-off look. Most books and magazines use even text. Although even text looks a little impersonal for letters to Mom, for newsletters and business correspondence, it can look quite sharp.

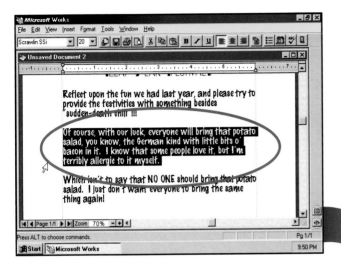

1 Select the text you want to make even.

NOTE ▼

Text that is even on both sides is called *justified* text.

2 Open the **Format** menu and select the **Paragraph** command. The Format Paragraph dialog box appears.

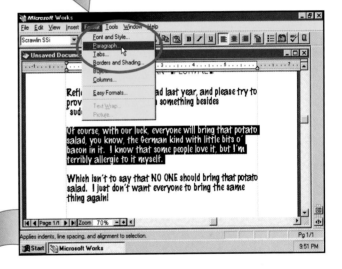

3 Click on the circle next to the word **Justified**. A black dot will appear in that circle to indicate that the option is selected.

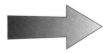

4 Click the **OK** button to enter your selection and make the dialog box go away.

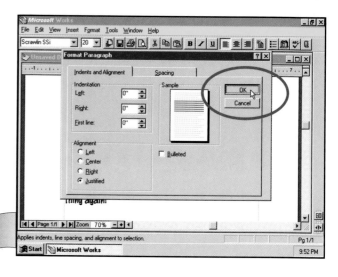

5 The selected text now appears even on both sides. The word processor does this by increasing the size of the spaces between words. Note that the last line of each paragraph doesn't go all the way to the right, so that the reader can still tell where the paragraph ends. ■

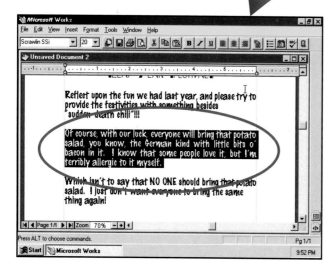

WHY WORRY?

Text that's even on both sides can be ugly when the spaces between words are too large. If you don't like the way the justified text looks, select the text and click the Left Align button to make it normal again!

Starting a New Page

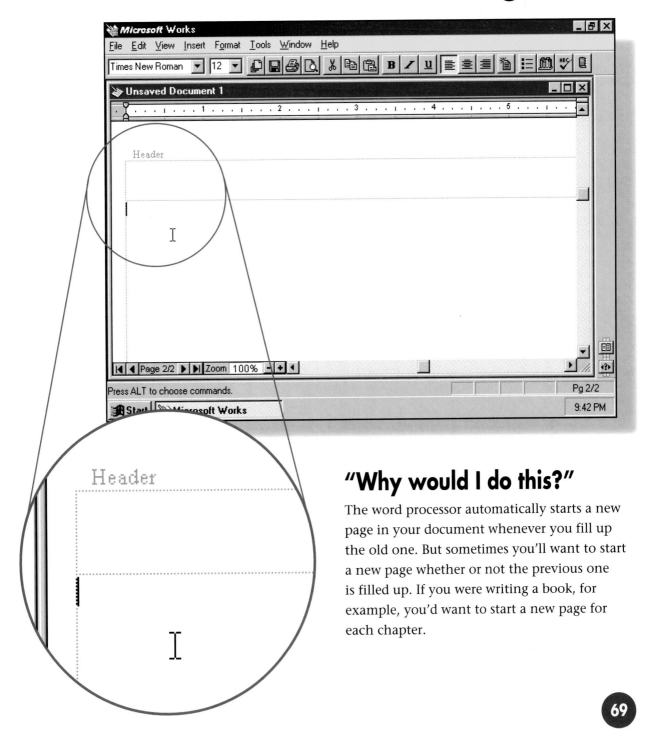

"Why would I do this?"

The word processor automatically starts a new page in your document whenever you fill up the old one. But sometimes you'll want to start a new page whether or not the previous one is filled up. If you were writing a book, for example, you'd want to start a new page for each chapter.

1 When you reach the point where you want to start a new page, pull down the **Insert** menu and select **Page Break**.

NOTE ▼

A shortcut for this is to hold down the Ctrl key and press Enter.

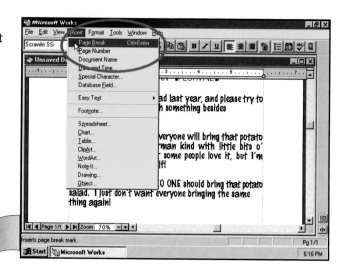

2 Works displays a new page and puts your cursor at the top of it. In addition, the page numbers displayed below the bottom left corner of the document each increase by one (the first number indicates the current page, and the second indicates the total number of pages).

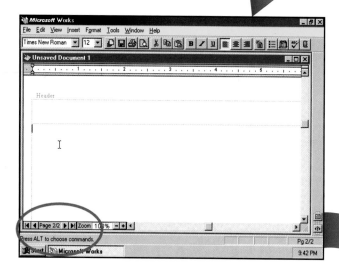

3 To remove a page break, put your cursor before the first character on the page and press the **Backspace** key (which may be marked **bkspc** or have a left-pointing arrow on it). ■

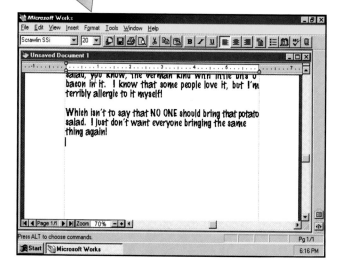

Changing Margins

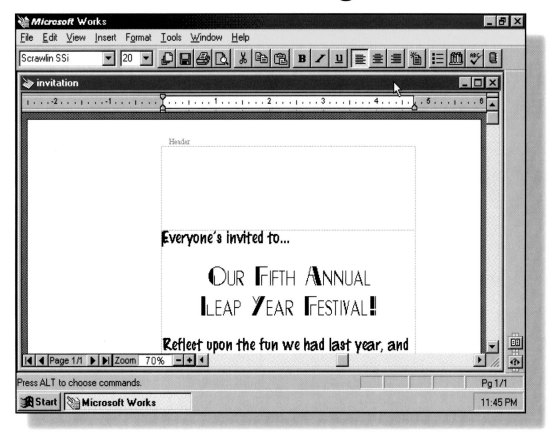

"Why would I do this?"

The margins are the white spaces that border your text; you cannot print beyond the margins. You might want to make your margins smaller if you're trying to fit as much as possible on each page. You might want to make them bigger if you are trying to create a more businesslike look.

1 Pull down the **File** menu and select the **Page Setup** command. The Page Setup dialog box appears so you can make your own changes.

> **NOTE** ▼
>
> This command changes the margins for all the pages in your document. (You cannot change the margins for an individual section or page.)

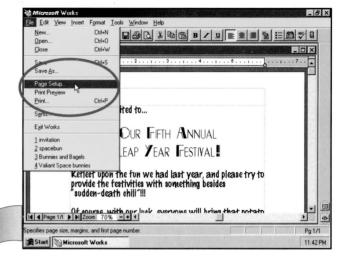

2 Works displays the existing margin settings (measured in inches) in the section marked Margins. Look in the Sample area to see a picture of what a full page of text looks like with these margins.

3 To increase the top margin size, click the up arrow button in the Top margin control. To decrease the size, click the down arrow button. The sample page size shows you what your page looks like with that setting.

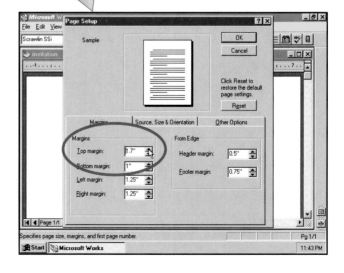

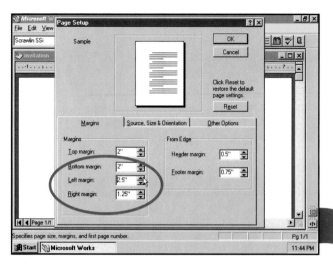

4 Adjust the bottom, left, and right margins in the same way.

5 Click the **OK** button to enter your selections and make the dialog box go away.

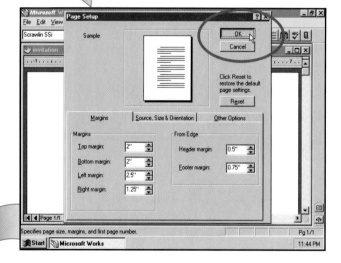

6 Your document now has the margins you entered. ■

WHY WORRY?

If you don't like the new margin setup, pull down the File menu and select Page Setup again. Click the Reset button and click OK to return to the previous margins!

Double-Spacing

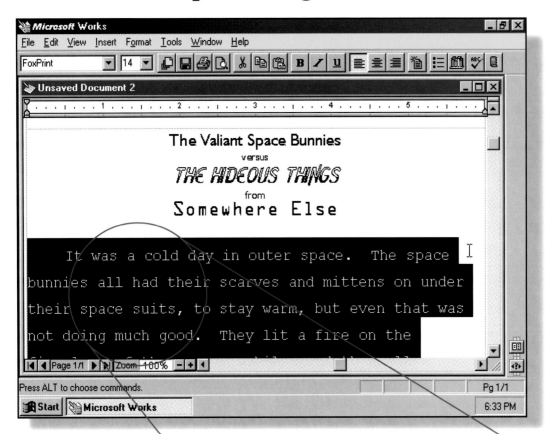

"Why would I do this?"

Double-spacing places a blank line after each line of text. If you're writing a story, a press release, or something else that someone is likely to edit by hand, it leaves room for that person to add editing marks.

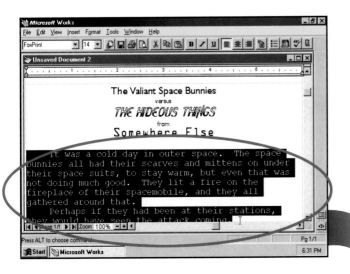

1 Select the text you want to double-space. (Alternatively, you can select nothing at all, and everything you type after you select the command will be double-spaced.)

NOTE ▼

It's usually better to type everything first and then make it double-spaced. By doing so, you are able to see more text on the screen at once, which makes it easier to spot mistakes and to move around your document.

2 Pull down the **Format** menu and select the **Paragraph** command. The Format Paragraph dialog box appears on the screen.

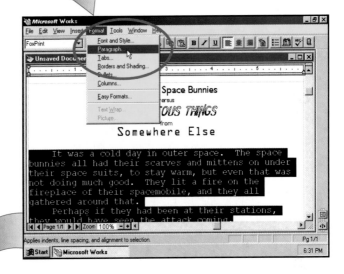

3 Click the **Spacing** tab to access the spacing controls.

4 Double-click on the up arrow next to the Line spacing box. The entry in the box changes to read 2li. This means "two lines," one line of text plus one blank line.

NOTE ▼

Using this control, you can put as many blank lines as you want after each line. Just remember that you want the number before the 1i to be one more than the number of blank lines.

5 Click the **OK** button to enter your selections and make the Format Paragraph dialog box go away.

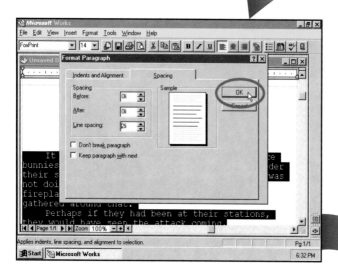

6 Your text is now double-spaced. You won't be able to put your cursor on the blank lines, only on the text lines. ■

WHY WORRY?

You can always go back to regular single-spacing. To do so, go through these steps again, except instead of clicking the up arrow by the Line spacing control, click the down arrow until the display says Auto.

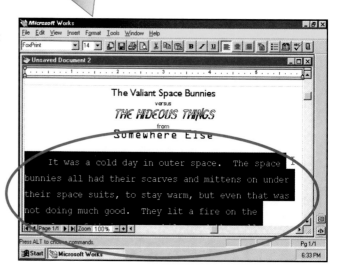

TASK 25
Adding a Picture

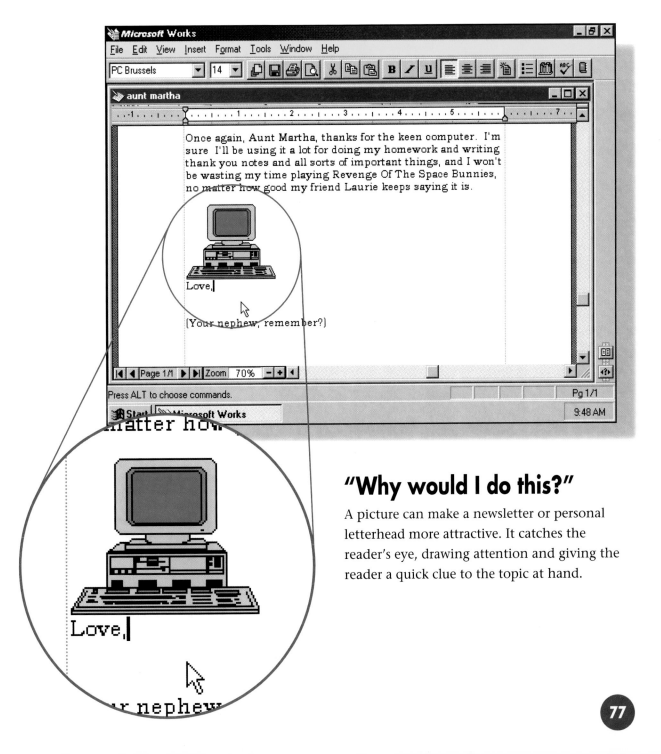

"Why would I do this?"

A picture can make a newsletter or personal letterhead more attractive. It catches the reader's eye, drawing attention and giving the reader a quick clue to the topic at hand.

1 Place the cursor where you want the picture to be.

> **NOTE** ▼
>
> You will probably want to put the picture on a new line without any text. Otherwise, you have to make the picture as small as the text, or you'll have a big gap between lines of text.

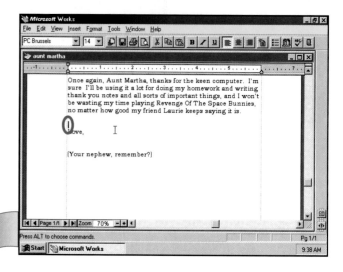

2 Pull down the **Insert** menu and select the **ClipArt** command.

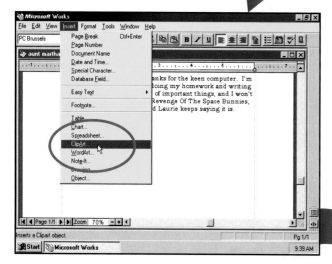

3 If you get this display, click the **OK** button to make it go away.

> **NOTE** ▼
>
> If you click the button next to "Quick tour of objects," Works leads you through a short explanation about putting pictures and other special things in your documents. If you never want to see this screen again, click the box marked "Don't display this message in the future" before you click the OK button.

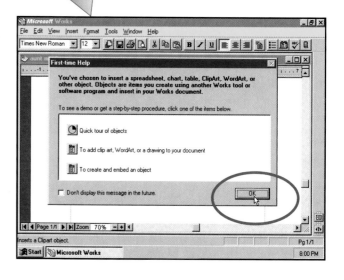

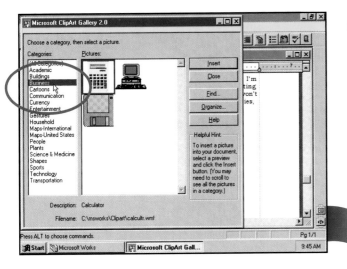

4 Click on the category of drawing you want, and the available drawings appear in the center column.

> **NOTE** ▼
> Works only comes with a few dozen drawings, but you can buy collections of clip art to add more.

5 Use the scroll bar if necessary to look through the drawings. When you see one you want, click on it, and a box appears around it.

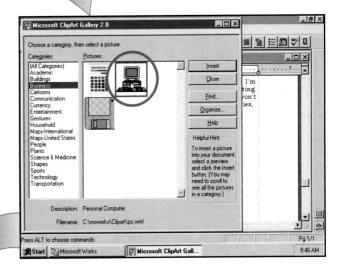

6 Click the **Insert** button.

> **NOTE** ▼
> If you decide you don't want to use any of the art, just click the Close button.

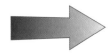

7 The art appears in your document with a series of gray squares and a gray box around it. Position the pointer over the square in the lower-right corner. The pointer changes to a square with two arrows above the word RESIZE.

NOTE ▼

The picture will only print in color if you have a color printer. Otherwise, it will print in black and white and gray.

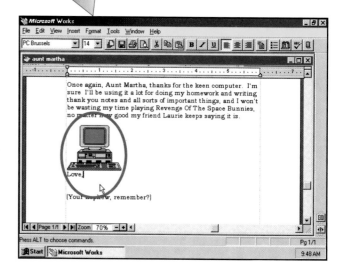

8 Press and hold the left mouse button. You now control the edge of the gray box, with which you can resize the picture. Move the mouse forward to make the picture smaller, or backward to make it bigger.

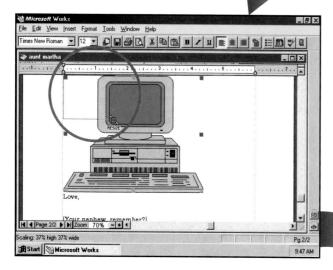

9 When the figure reaches the desired size, release the left mouse button. Works resizes the picture accordingly. ■

WHY WORRY?

If you want to get rid of the picture, just click on it to select it and press the Delete key. The picture disappears!

TASK 26
Finding a Word or Phrase

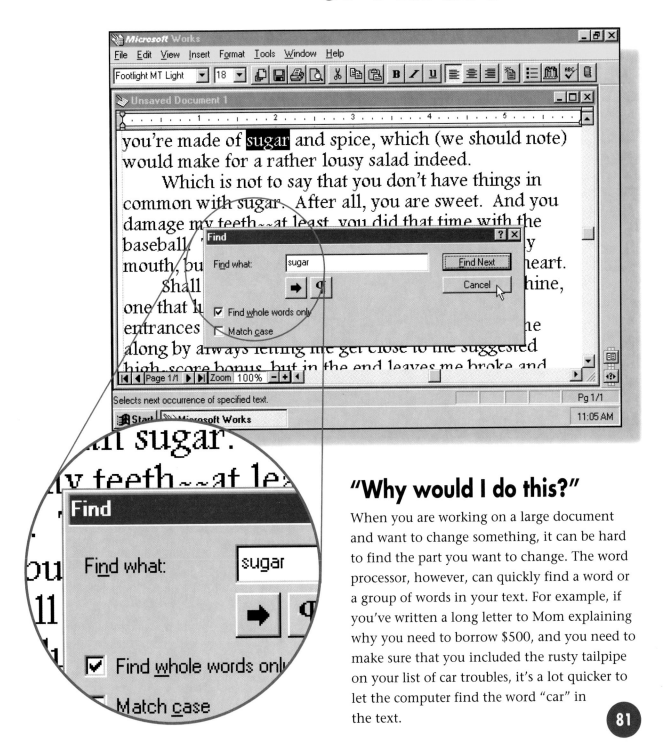

"Why would I do this?"

When you are working on a large document and want to change something, it can be hard to find the part you want to change. The word processor, however, can quickly find a word or a group of words in your text. For example, if you've written a long letter to Mom explaining why you need to borrow $500, and you need to make sure that you included the rusty tailpipe on your list of car troubles, it's a lot quicker to let the computer find the word "car" in the text.

81

1 Hold down the **Ctrl** key and press the **Home** key. This moves the cursor to the left of the very first character of your document. Be careful not to accidentally select any text.

> **NOTE** ▼
>
> If you do have text selected, Works searches only the part that's selected for the word you want.

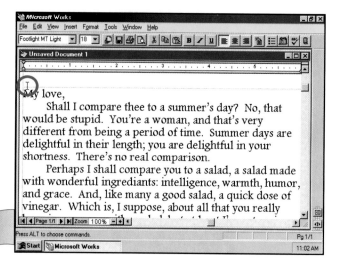

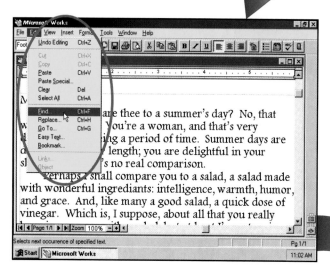

2 Pull down the **Edit** menu and select the **Find** command.

> **NOTE** ▼
>
> A quick shortcut for this is to hold down the Ctrl key and press F.

3 In the Find dialog box, type the word or phrase you want to look for.

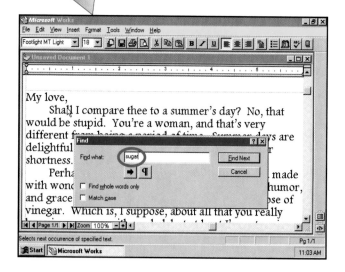

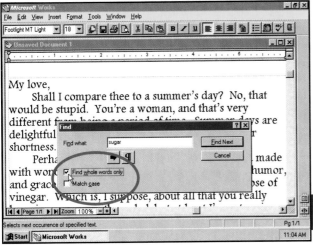

4 Click the **Find whole words only** box if you want to prevent Works from finding the specified word in the middle of another word (such as "cat" in "catalog" or "Piscataway"). However, you'll also miss finding it in places where it does mean "cat," like in the word "cats."

NOTE ▼

If you used this option in your last search, there may already be a check mark in the box. To turn the option off, click the box again, and the check mark disappears.

5 Click the **Find Next** button, and Works finds and highlights the first occurrence of the word.

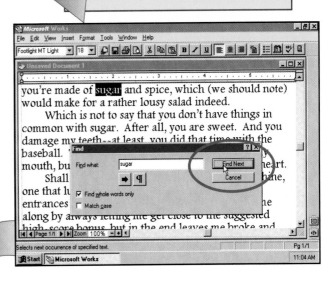

6 If this is what you are looking for, click the **Cancel** button. The Find dialog box goes away, and you can continue editing your document. Otherwise, click the **Find Next** button again, and the search continues.

7 When the word processor comes to the end of the document, it asks you if it should continue searching from the beginning of the document. Click the **No** button.

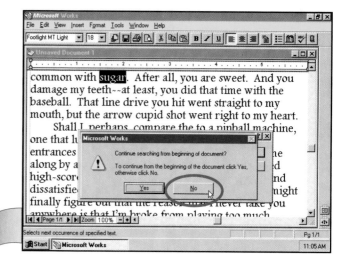

8 If you try to continue searching after Works has found every occurrence of the word in the document, Works tells you that it did not find a match. Click the **OK** button, and then click **Cancel** to make the Find dialog box go away. ■

NOTE ▼

If Works did not find the word in the document at all, consider these three possible reasons. The word may not be in the document; you may have accidentally had text selected when you began searching; or you may have misspelled the word. If you're pretty sure the word is there, try the search again!

Checking Your Spelling

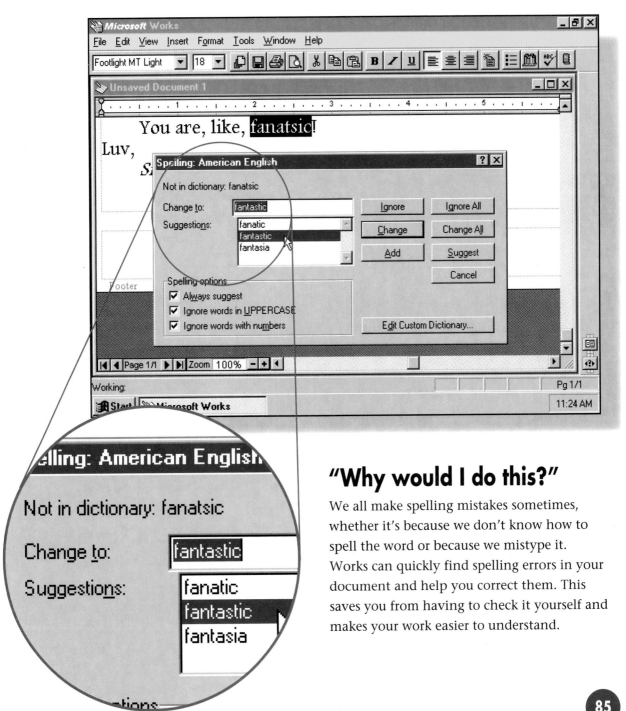

"Why would I do this?"

We all make spelling mistakes sometimes, whether it's because we don't know how to spell the word or because we mistype it. Works can quickly find spelling errors in your document and help you correct them. This saves you from having to check it yourself and makes your work easier to understand.

1 To check your whole document, make sure no text is selected. To check a section of your document, select that section. To check just one word you're unsure of, select that word.

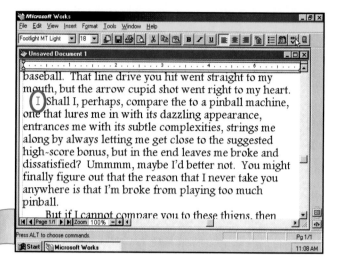

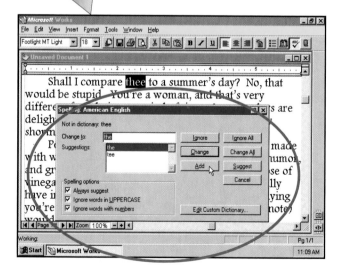

2 Click the **Spell Check** button, and Works starts checking your document for misspelled words.

NOTE ▼

The Spell Check will only find misspelled words, it won't be able to tell if you've typed the wrong word. For example, if you type "act" when you mean to type "cat," Works won't spot the error because "act" is a word.

3 When Works finds a word it doesn't recognize, it highlights the word and displays the Spelling dialog box. Here you see the word it doesn't recognize, the word it thinks you meant, and a list of other words you might have meant.

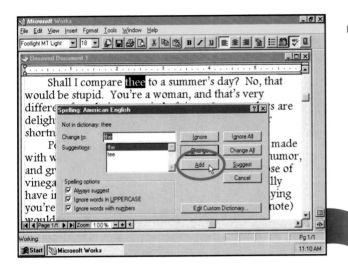

4 If the word Works doesn't recognize is actually spelled correctly (if it is a name or an uncommon word, for example), click the **Add** button. Works adds this word to its dictionary so it will recognize it in the future. Works then continues checking your document.

NOTE ▼

If you don't want to add the word to the dictionary, click the Ignore button instead of the Add button.

5 If you want to replace the misspelled word with a word other than the one in the Change to box, look at the Suggestions list. If you find the correct word there, click on it, and it appears in the Change to box.

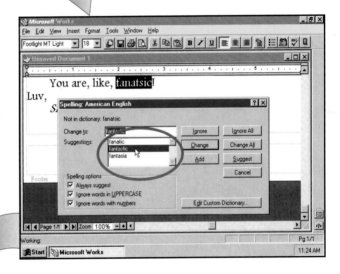

6 If the correct word isn't in the Suggestions list, type the correct word in the Change to box.

7 With the correct word in the Change to box, click the **Change All** button. Works continues to go through the document, and automatically replaces this misspelled word with the word you've selected every time it appears.

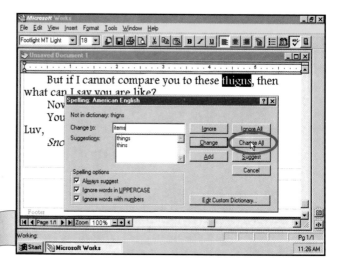

> **NOTE** ▼
>
> If you want Works to replace only the first occurrence of the error, click the Change button instead of Change All. The next time Works finds this same misspelled word in the document, it asks you again what you want to do about it.

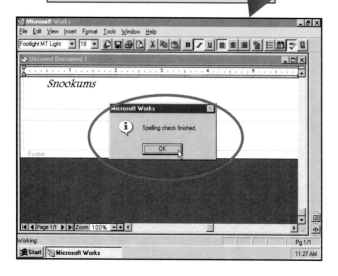

8 When Works finishes checking your document, it tells you Spelling check finished. Click the **OK** button to continue working on your document.

> **WHY WORRY?**
>
> If Works starts checking your spelling, and you decide you don't want to continue the check, wait until it finds a word it doesn't recognize. Then click the Cancel button, and Works stops the spell check.

Printing Your Document

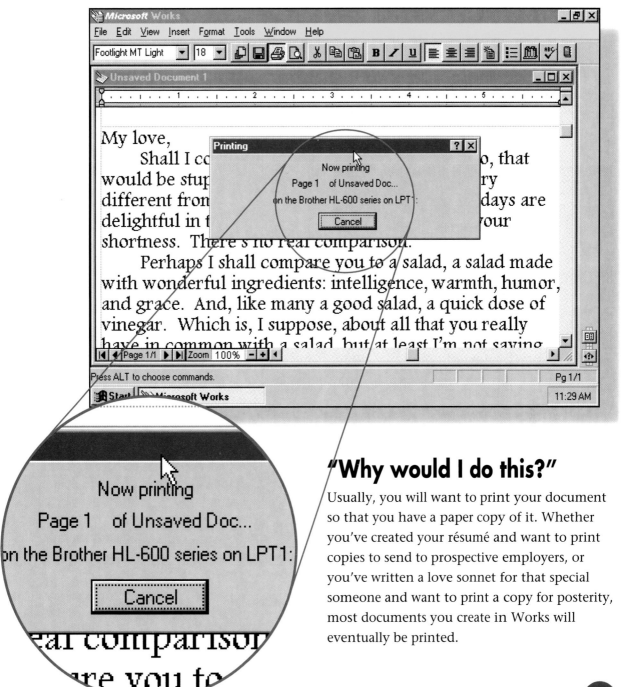

"Why would I do this?"

Usually, you will want to print your document so that you have a paper copy of it. Whether you've created your résumé and want to print copies to send to prospective employers, or you've written a love sonnet for that special someone and want to print a copy for posterity, most documents you create in Works will eventually be printed.

1 Make sure that your printer is turned on and it has enough paper.

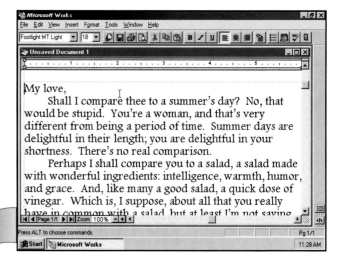

2 Click the **Print** button.

NOTE ▼

If you want more control over printing, pull down the File menu and select the Print command to bring up the Print dialog box. It has settings with which you control which individual pages you want to print, whether you want multiple copies, and other printing particulars.

3 Excel displays this box to let you know the document is being sent to the printer. When the box disappears, you can go back to working on your document (even if the printer is not done printing yet). ■

WHY WORRY?

If you start printing a document and want to stop, just click the Cancel button!

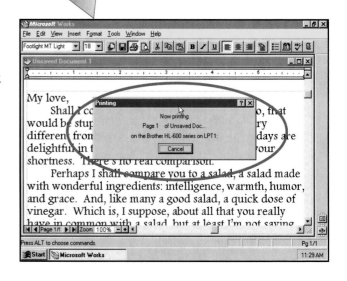

Saving Your Document

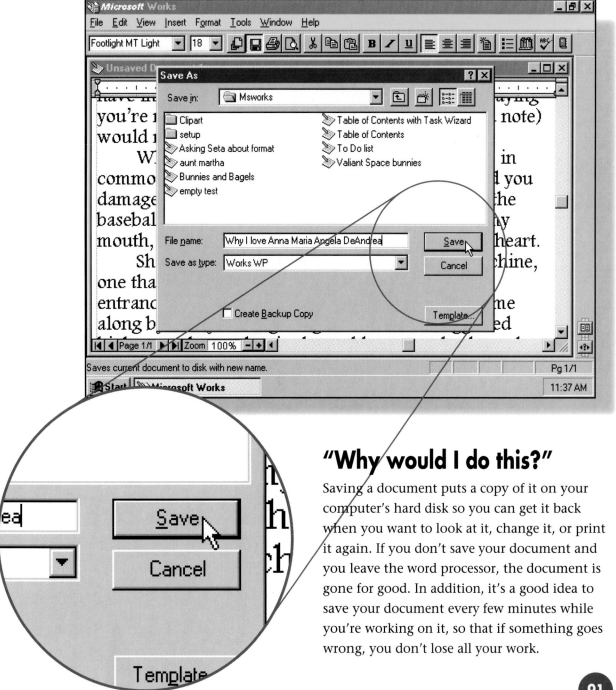

"Why would I do this?"

Saving a document puts a copy of it on your computer's hard disk so you can get it back when you want to look at it, change it, or print it again. If you don't save your document and you leave the word processor, the document is gone for good. In addition, it's a good idea to save your document every few minutes while you're working on it, so that if something goes wrong, you don't lose all your work.

1 Click the **Save** button on the toolbar. If you loaded this document from the disk or have already saved it to the disk, Works saves it, replacing the copy that was already on the disk with this one. You can continue working with your file.

NOTE ▼

To save the document without wiping out the previous copy, don't click the Save button. Instead, pull down the File menu and select the Save As command. Give the document a different name from that of the old version.

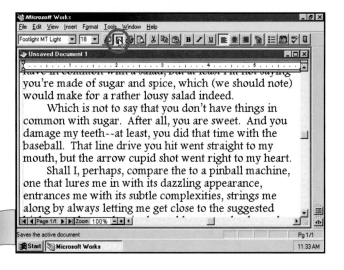

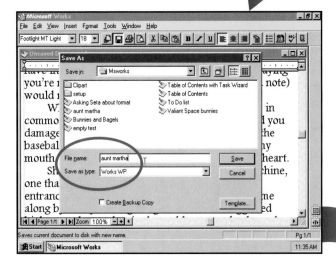

2 If you have not saved this document before, the Save As dialog box appears. Type a name for the document in the File name box (where "aunt martha" is in this figure). Make sure it's a name that you can recognize, and that it is different from the name of any other document.

NOTE ▼

The name can be up to 256 letters, numbers, and spaces long. Some document listings show only the first 25 characters, though, so make sure you can recognize it from that.

3 Click the **Save** button, and Works saves the document to the disk.

WHY WORRY?

If you decide that you don't want to save the file, just click the Cancel button and continue working on your document.

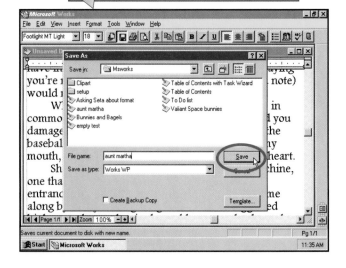

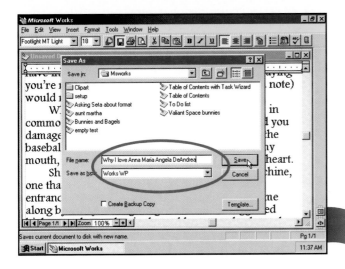

4 If Works tells you the file name already exists, you cannot use the name because you have already used it for another document. Click the **No** button. Type in a different name and click the **Save** button.

5 The name that you gave the document appears at the top of the document, and you can continue working with it.

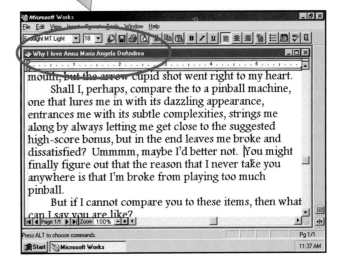

TASK 30

Leaving the Word Processor

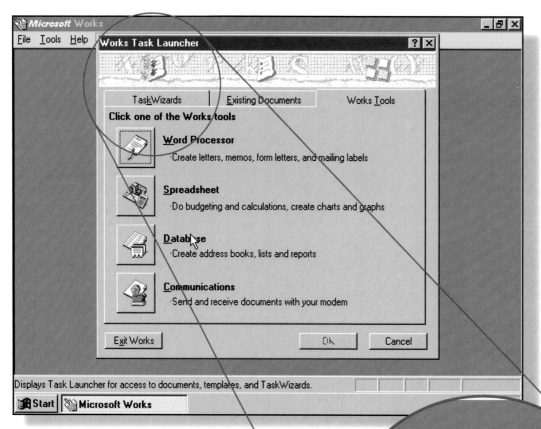

"Why would I do this?"

When you have finished working with your document, you'll want to leave the word processor so you can open another document, get into some other part of Works, or leave Works altogether.

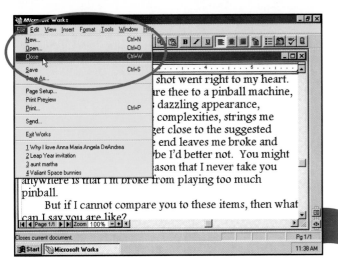

1 Pull down the **File** menu and select the **Close** command.

> **NOTE** ▼
>
> Works provides two shortcuts for doing this: hold down the Ctrl key and press W, or double-click on the picture of a pencil and paper that's next to the document name.

2 If you have made changes to the file since you last saved it, Works asks if you want to save changes to this document. Click the **Yes** button if you do, and Works saves the document to disk just as it would if you used the Save command. Click **No** if you want Works to forget those changes.

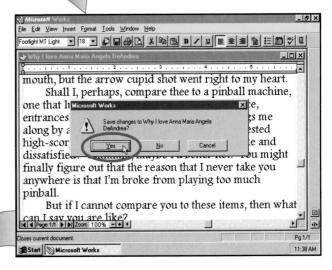

3 The Task Launcher screen appears. From here, you can launch any other part of Works or exit Works altogether. ■

> **WHY WORRY?**
>
> If you save your document and then decide that you aren't done working with it, just load it again and get back to work.

PART III

Using the Spreadsheet

A spreadsheet enables you to do with numbers what a word processor enables you to do with words. You put together numbers and equations, and then change them around whenever you need to. You can move and copy numbers, and change and reuse equations. You can input a lot of information and equations based on that information, and the program will automatically figure out the results of those equations.

For example, if you're planning to paint some rooms in your house, you can use the spreadsheet to calculate how much paint you need. You simply enter the necessary information: the dimensions of each room and how many square feet a can of paint covers. One equation uses a room's dimensions to figure out how many square feet of wall and ceiling space are in that room. Another equation uses the result of the first equation and the information about how much each can of paint covers to figure out how many cans of paint that room requires. And if you change any of that information, the spreadsheet automatically recalculates the equations.

A spreadsheet is a big grid that looks like a humongous tic-tac-toe board. A line of squares across is called a *row*, and a line of squares up-and-down is called a *column*. Each row is identified by a number: row 1, row 2, row 3, and so on. Each column is identified by a letter: column A, column B, and so on. If you have more than 26 columns, the spreadsheet identifies them by two letters. So next to column Z is column AA, then AB, and so on through AZ; after that comes BA, and so on. The squares where rows and columns connect are called *cells*. Each cell is identified by a cell address, which is made up of the column letter and row number. So the cell in the upper-left corner is cell A1. Next to A1 is B1, and below B1 is B2.

Into each of these squares, you can put a number (information for calculations), an equation, or a word label to help identify what the numbers and equations are for. The program provides a lot of tools that make it easy to change your information, your equations, and the way they look, and it can even draw graphs for you.

A spreadsheet can be very large, with hundreds of columns and thousands of rows. There's no way that you can show all of that on the screen at once. In the same way that the word processor shows you only part of a page at the time, Works shows you only part of the spreadsheet. Usually, it shows you 16 rows and 8 columns at a time—a single rectangular part of the full spreadsheet. However, you can move around the spreadsheet, changing which set of rows and columns you are looking at.

Works even has predesigned spreadsheets for things like calculating loan payments and keeping track of employee hours and pay. To use a prepared spreadsheet, all you have to do is enter the information. If you need to do certain calculations regularly but you're not good at figuring out how to do those calculations, you only need to get someone to help you once. That person sets up the equations once, and then you just reuse the spreadsheet and enter different information each time.

Once you're comfortable using the basic spreadsheet tools described in this chapter, use Works' Help system to learn some of the advanced tools. You can learn details about what the fancy mathematical functions can do for you. There's information about how to print out just part of a spreadsheet. You can change the size of the letters and numbers used and even use color to make your printed spreadsheet look sharp. You don't have to learn all of these things at once; just do a little exploring when you think of something you'd like to learn.

TASK 31

Creating a New, Blank Spreadsheet

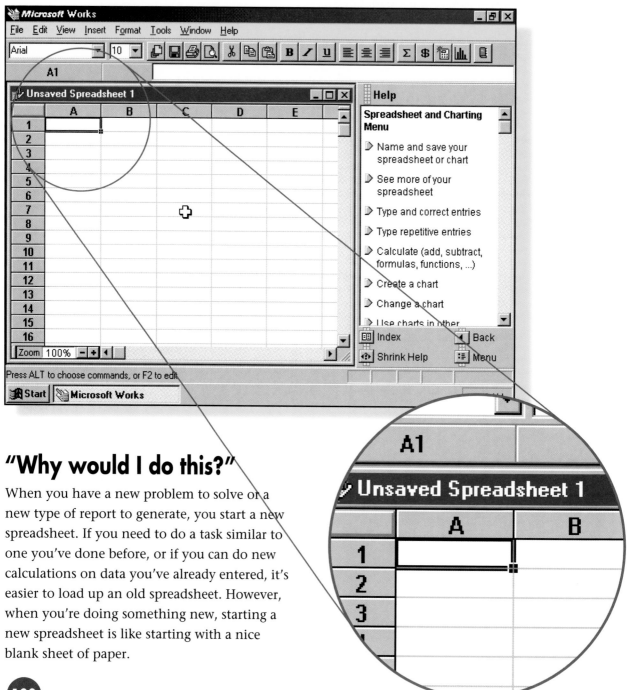

"Why would I do this?"

When you have a new problem to solve or a new type of report to generate, you start a new spreadsheet. If you need to do a task similar to one you've done before, or if you can do new calculations on data you've already entered, it's easier to load up an old spreadsheet. However, when you're doing something new, starting a new spreadsheet is like starting with a nice blank sheet of paper.

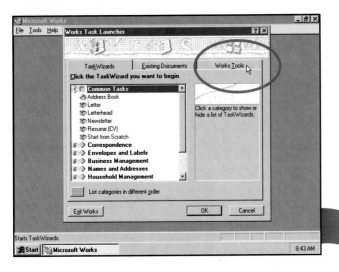

1 On the Task Launcher screen, click on the **Works Tools** tab. Works displays a set of buttons, one for each of the main programs it provides.

2 Click on the **Spreadsheet** button.

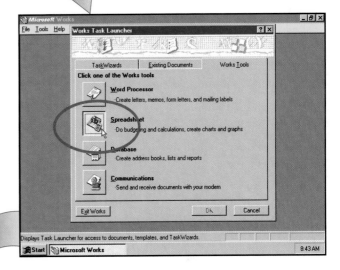

3 Works starts the spreadsheet program and displays a blank spreadsheet. The white area of the screen is your actual spreadsheet. The rest of the screen has tools you can use to input and work with the data and equations in your spreadsheet. ■

Retrieving a Spreadsheet You've Already Made

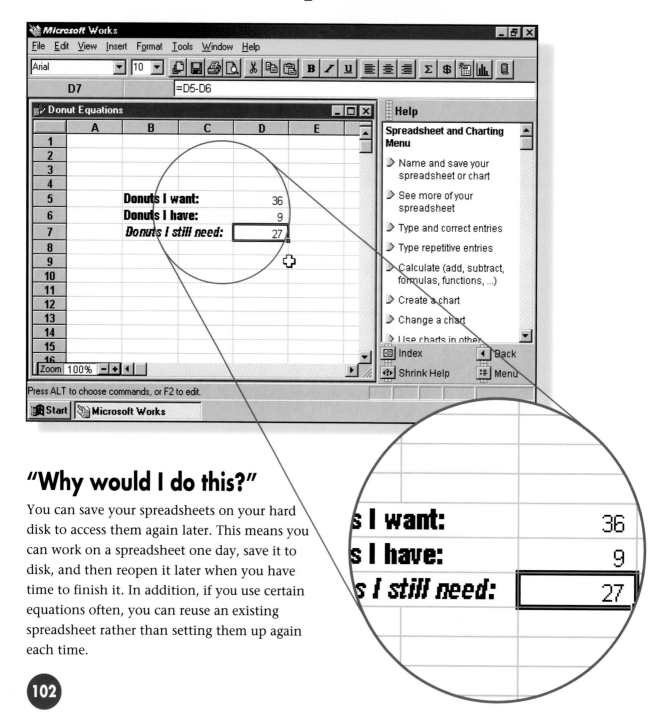

"Why would I do this?"

You can save your spreadsheets on your hard disk to access them again later. This means you can work on a spreadsheet one day, save it to disk, and then reopen it later when you have time to finish it. In addition, if you use certain equations often, you can reuse an existing spreadsheet rather than setting them up again each time.

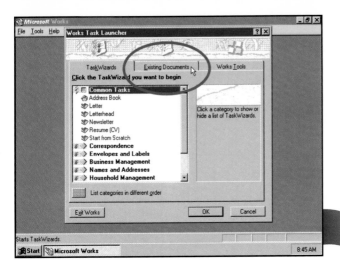

1 On the Task Launcher screen, click on the **Existing Documents** tab. Works displays a list of documents you've worked with recently.

2 Find the name of the spreadsheet you are looking for and double-click on it. (The spreadsheet documents have a picture of a calculator and a pad next to the name.) Works starts the spreadsheet program and displays the spreadsheet you selected.

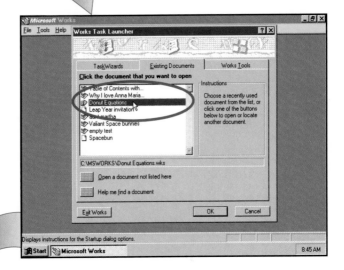

3 If you cannot find your spreadsheet on that list, click on the **Open a document not listed here** button.

4 Works displays the Open dialog box, which contains a more complete list of spreadsheets and other items. If you see your spreadsheet there, double-click on it.

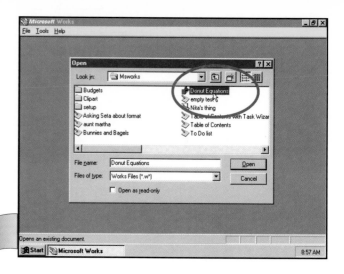

5 If you stored the spreadsheet in a folder, open the Look in list and double-click on that folder's name. Works updates the list of documents to show the contents of the folder you selected. Double-click on the name of your spreadsheet.

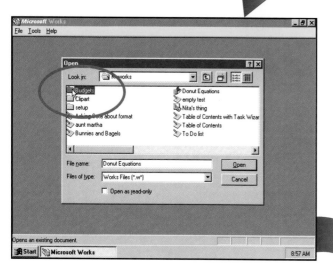

NOTE ▼

The Look in box indicates which folder you're looking in. If that's not the folder you want, click on the button just to the right. This brings you up out of that folder.

6 The spreadsheet you chose appears on the screen, ready for you to edit. ■

WHY WORRY?

If you open the wrong spreadsheet, just close it without saving it. It doesn't mess up the wrong spreadsheet, and you can go back to the Task Launcher to get the right one!

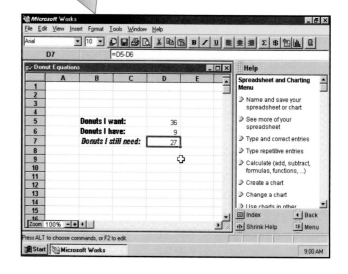

Moving Around the Spreadsheet

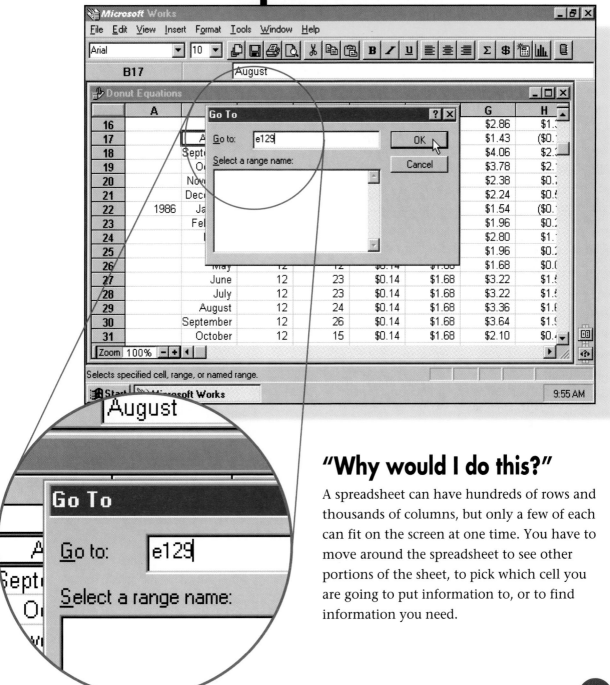

"Why would I do this?"

A spreadsheet can have hundreds of rows and thousands of columns, but only a few of each can fit on the screen at one time. You have to move around the spreadsheet to see other portions of the sheet, to pick which cell you are going to put information to, or to find information you need.

1 On the spreadsheet, there is a dark black box around the currently selected cell. The cell address of the selected cell appears in a box just above and to the left of the spreadsheet.

NOTE ▼

When you start a brand new spreadsheet, cell A1 (in the upper-left corner) is always the selected cell. When you retrieve an existing spreadsheet, whichever cell was selected when you saved it is still selected.

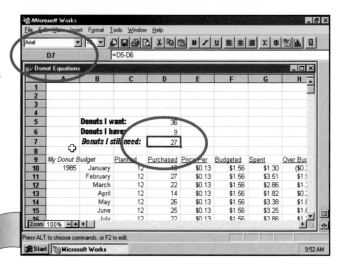

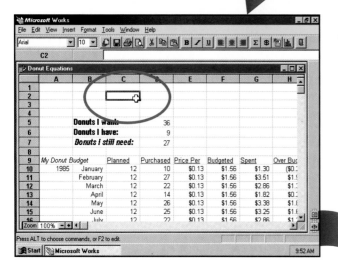

2 To select any other cell, move your pointer (which looks like a big plus sign) to that cell. Click on the cell, and the dark box surrounds it to show that it has been selected.

NOTE ▼

To select a cell that's not visible in the working area, use the scroll bars to bring it into view, and then click on it.

3 Press the left arrow key to move the box one cell to the left and select that cell. Likewise, the right arrow key moves the box one cell to the right, the up arrow key moves it up one cell, and the down arrow key moves it down one cell.

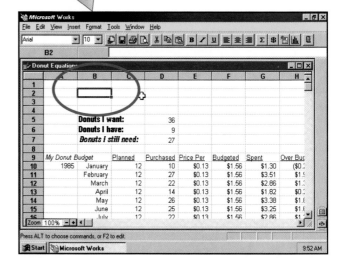

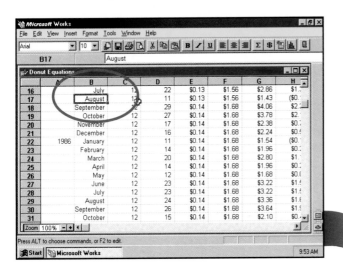

4 Press the **Page Down** (or **PgDn**) key to move the selection box down the spreadsheet a whole screen's worth and display that area. The **Page Up** (or **PgUp**) key moves the box up one full screen.

NOTE ▼

A shortcut for this command is to hold down the Ctrl key and press G.

5 To go quickly to a specific cell, pull down the **Edit** menu and select the **Go To** command.

WHY WORRY?

If you get lost, hold down the Ctrl key and hit the Home key. Works returns you to the upper-left corner of the spreadsheet and selects cell A1.

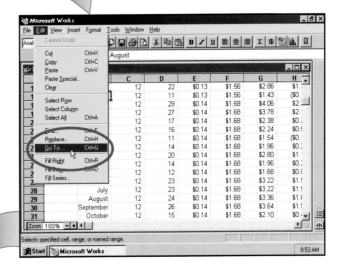

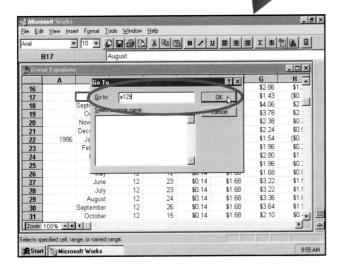

6 The Go To dialog box appears. Type the address (column letter, then row number) of the cell you want to go to and click on **OK**. Works displays that cell, which is now selected. ■

Selecting a Range of Cells

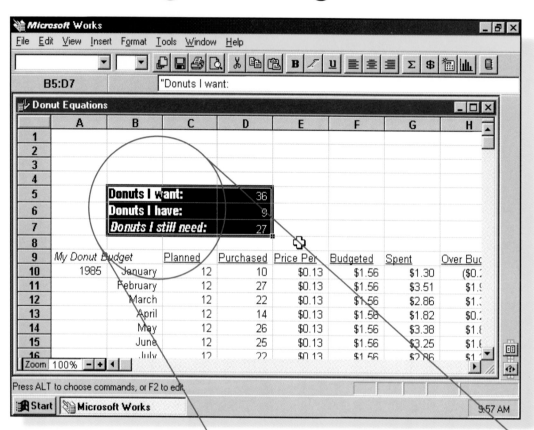

"Why would I do this?"

Sometimes you will want to perform a task that
affects a rectangular range of cells. You might
want to copy them all to another place, or you
might want to add up all the numbers in those
cells and put the answer in another cell, for
example. You select the range to tell Works
which cells you want your commands to affect.

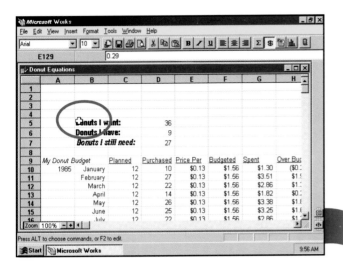

1 Place your pointer on the cell in the upper-left corner of the range you want to select.

> **NOTE** ▼
>
> A *range* has to be a single rectangle of cells.

2 Press and hold the left mouse button and drag the pointer to the lower-right corner of the rectangle. An outline box surrounds the entire rectangle, and all but one of the cells become highlighted (white text on a black background).

> **NOTE** ▼
>
> You can actually start at any corner of the rectangle and drag the mouse to the opposite corner. The cell that isn't highlighted will be in the corner where you started.

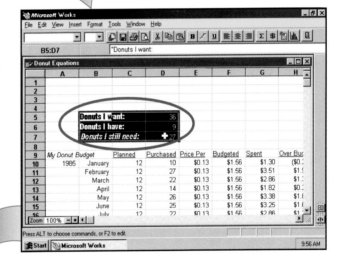

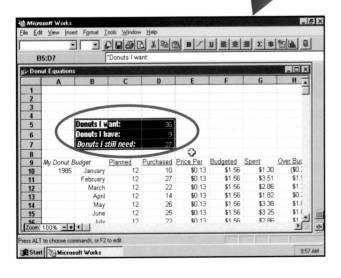

3 Release the mouse button. The range of cells is selected. Works displays the *range address* (the cell addresses of the upper-left and lower-right cells in the range, separated by a colon) in the box above the upper-left corner of the spreadsheet. ■

TASK 35
Entering Numbers

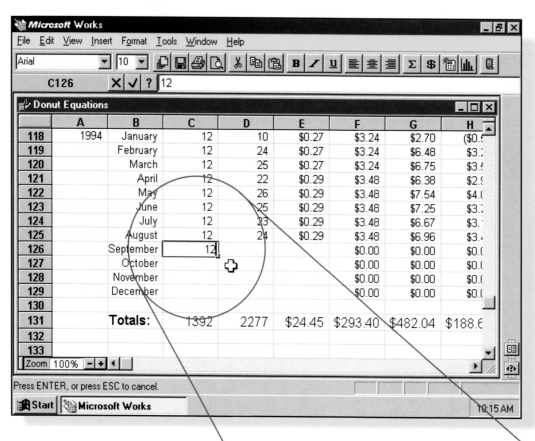

"Why would I do this?"

Before a spreadsheet can perform calculations or create graphs, you must enter the numbers you want it to calculate or graph. You type each number into its own cell.

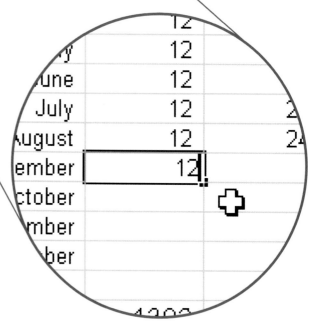

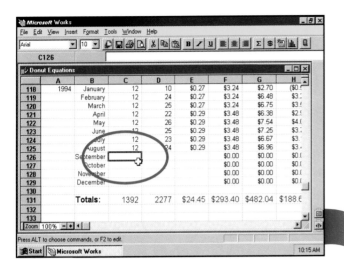

1 Select the cell in which you want to type a number. The black selection box surrounds that cell to show that it is selected.

2 Type the number that you want to enter. As you type it, the number appears on the editing line and in the cell. The outline around the cell thins.

NOTE ▼

Be careful not to use the lowercase letter l and the uppercase letter O instead of the 1 and 0. They may look the same, but the computer won't understand them.

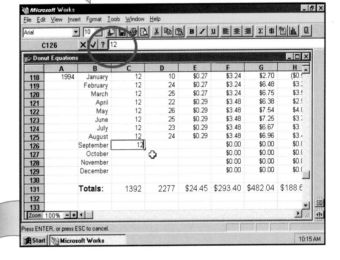

3 When you finish typing the number, press the right arrow key (to move to the next cell across) or the down arrow key (to move to the next cell down). Works enters the number in the selected cell and clears it from the editing line. ■

WHY WORRY?

To delete the most recent entry, select the Edit Undo Entry command.

Entering an Equation

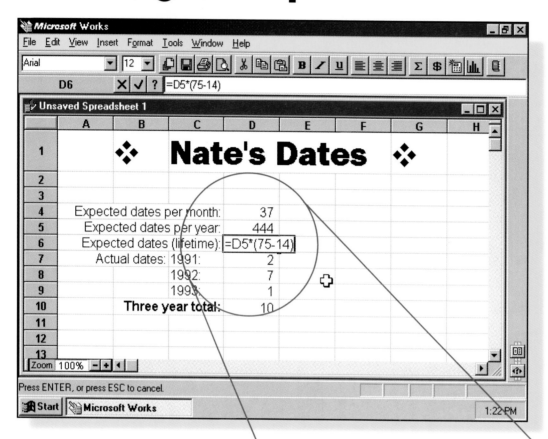

"Why Would I Do This?"

A spreadsheet can calculate things for you quickly and easily. But you must type an equation into a cell to tell the spreadsheet what calculation you want it to perform. Your equations can include numbers or references to numbers in other cells. If you include a reference to another cell and then change the cell you've referenced, Works automatically changes the result of the equation that contains the reference.

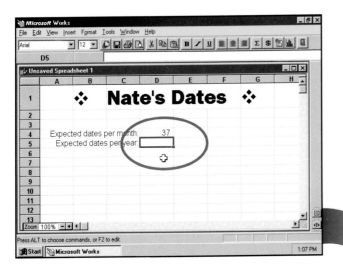

1 Select the cell in which you want to enter the equation.

2 Type = to tell Works you're entering an equation. The thick outline around the cell turns into a thin outline. The equals sign appears in the selected cell and on the editing line. There is a blinking cursor after it in the cell.

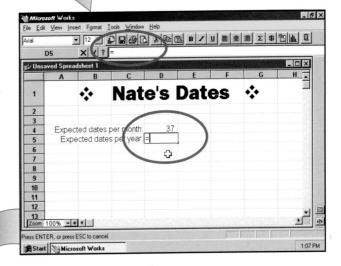

3 Type the first figure of your equation. For example, if you want to calculate 15 times 27, type the number **15**. If you want the first figure to be the value of another cell, type in its cell address. For example, to calculate the value of cell D7 times 12, type **D7**.

113

4 Another way of putting a cell address into your equation is to click on that cell. The cell you click on becomes highlighted, and its cell address appears in the equation as white type on a blue background.

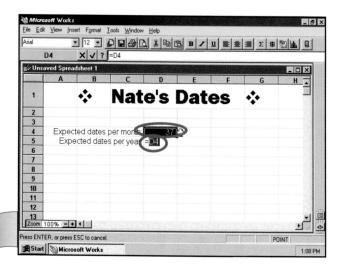

5 To add, type +. To subtract, type –. To multiply, type *. To divide, type /. The operator you type appears in your equation. In this figure, I typed * to multiply the number of dates per month by 12 months.

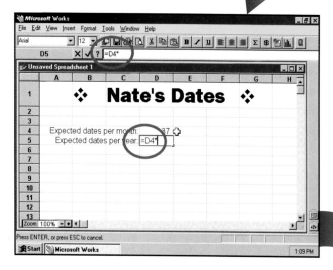

NOTE ▼

If you clicked on a cell to add its address to your equation, that cell now looks normal (it's no longer high-lighted), and the cell reference looks normal instead of being white text on blue.

6 Type the second number or cell address. For example, if you're calculating D4 times 12, type **12**. Again, if you want to add a cell address instead, simply click on the cell.

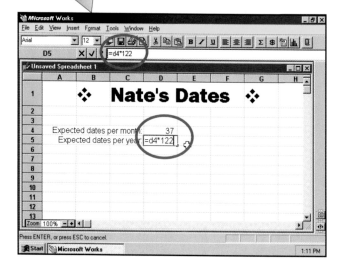

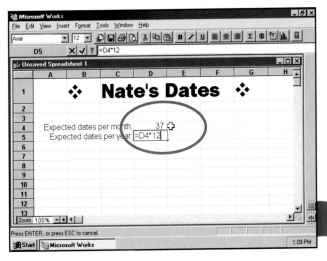

7 You can correct typing mistakes in your equation as you work. Use the **Backspace** key (marked "bkspc" or with an arrow pointing to the left) to remove characters. Type normally to add characters. All changes you make within the cell also appear in the equation shown in the editing line.

8 Keep adding math operators and numbers or cell references as necessary to make a more complex equation (such as D7+D8+D9).

NOTE

The spreadsheet calculates things inside parentheses first. For example, (D5*75)−14 means "multiply the value in cell D5 by 75, and then subtract 14 from the result." The result of that equation is different from the result of D5*(75−14), which means "subtract 14 from 75, and then multiply the result by the value in D5."

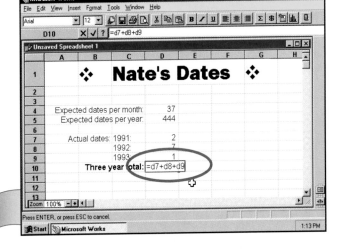

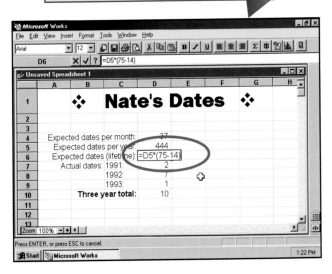

9 If you have more than one math operator, use parentheses to show the order in which you want the operations performed.

10 When you finish entering the equation, hit **Enter** to tell Works that the equation is ready. Once again the cell has the thick outline around it, but now it contains the answer to the equation! The editing line, however, still contains the equation.

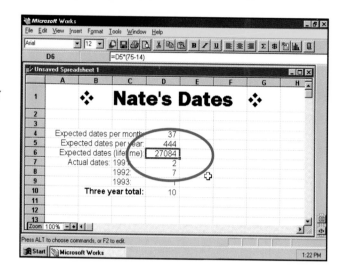

NOTE ▼

You can end the equation and move to the next cell by hitting one of the cursor arrow keys instead of Enter.

WHY WORRY?

If you made a mistake typing the equation, just double-click on the cell. The equation reappears in the cell, and you can edit it as normal.

TASK 37

Using a Function

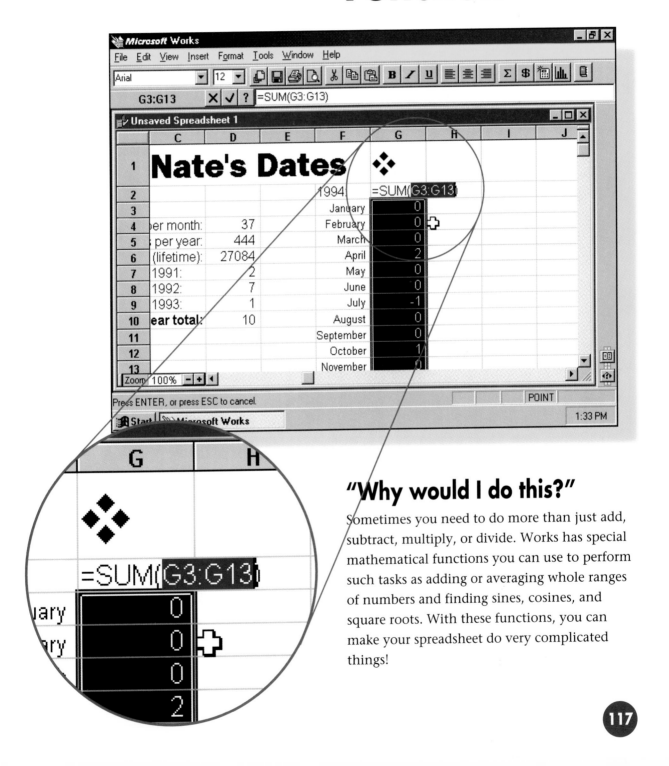

"Why would I do this?"

Sometimes you need to do more than just add, subtract, multiply, or divide. Works has special mathematical functions you can use to perform such tasks as adding or averaging whole ranges of numbers and finding sines, cosines, and square roots. With these functions, you can make your spreadsheet do very complicated things!

117

1 Select the cell into which you want to enter the formula.

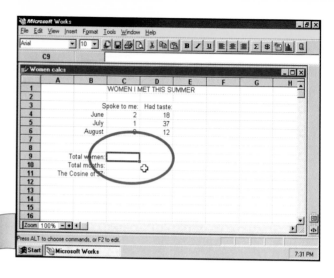

2 Pull down the **Insert** menu and select the **Function** command.

NOTE ▼

All the functions are listed in alphabetical order. If you want to look at a specific type of functions only, click on the white circle (called an *option button*) next to the function type you want in the Category list.

3 Works displays the Insert Function dialog box, which contains a list of available functions. Use the scroll bar to scroll through the list and find the function you are looking for.

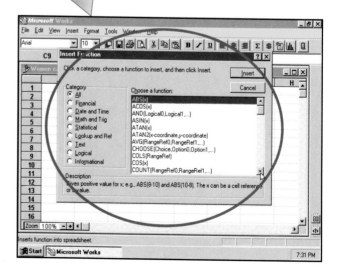

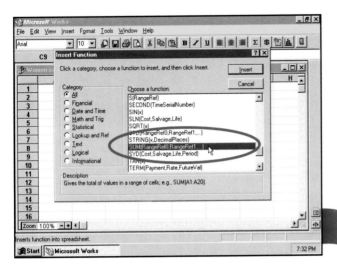

4 Click on the function you want to use. That function becomes highlighted, and a description of it appears in the Description box.

NOTE ▼

If you read the description and decide this isn't the function you want, scroll through the list to find another function you think will do, and click on that. If you don't want to select a function, click on the Cancel button.

5 With the correct function selected, click on the **Insert** button. The Insert Function dialog box disappears. In this example, we have selected the SUM function, which adds together all the cells in a range.

NOTE ▼

The SUM function is the function you'll use the most. It's good for totalling rows or columns of numbers.

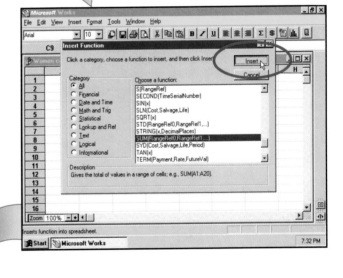

6 The SUM function appears in the cell and in the editing box. Part of the function is a set of parentheses with `RangeRef0`, `RangeRef1,...` between them. This is a placeholder that you will replace with the address of the cell range that you want to add together. Part of the placeholder is highlighted (white text on blue).

7 Put your pointer before the first R in `RangeRef0`. Hold down the mouse button and drag your mouse right until all of `RangeRef0,RangeRef1,...` is in blue. Make sure the parentheses before and after this aren't blue. Release the mouse button.

NOTE ▼

You can also indicate the range by typing the cell address of the upper-left corner cell, typing a colon (:), and then typing the address of the lower-right corner cell.

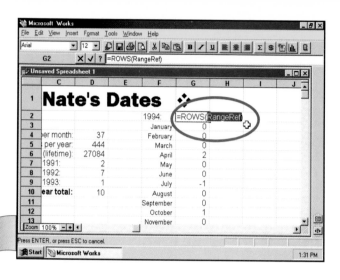

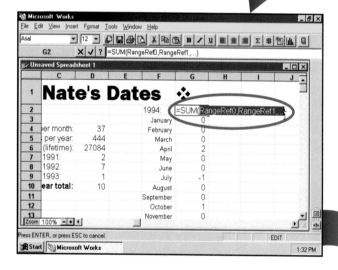

8 Select the range you want to use by dragging your mouse from one corner of the range to the diagonally opposite corner. The address of the cell range replaces the placeholder both in the cell and on the editing line.

NOTE ▼

To enter a negative number, type a minus sign, then the number. To enter a negative number, type a minus sign, then the number.

9 Press **Enter**. The formula remains on the editing line, and the result of the calculation appears in the cell.

WHY WORRY?

If you made a mistake in the formula, double-click on the cell. Now you can edit it just like an equation.

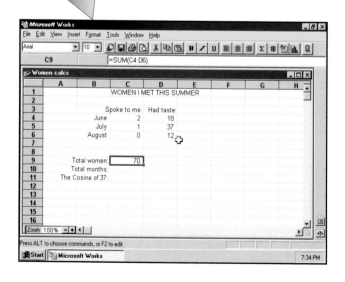

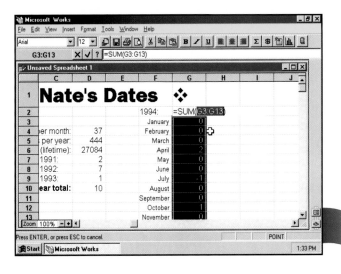

10 Other functions have different placeholders. If a placeholder is just RangeRef, highlight **RangeRef** and then select a cell range (just as you did for RangeRef0,RangeRef1,...).

11 If the placeholder is anything else, it's holding the place for a single value. Highlight the placeholder. Then either type in a number for the calculation, or click on a cell whose value you want to use.

> **NOTE** ▼
>
> The placeholder is either an X or a word describing the value it's holding the place for. For example, if you're doing a financial calculation, the placeholder for an interest rate will say Rate.

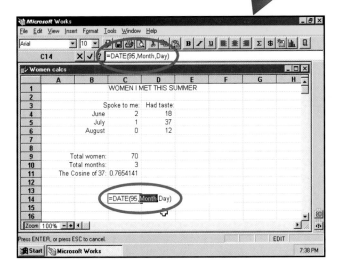

12 RangeRef0,RangeRef1,... is the only placeholder with commas in it. If the function has several items separated by commas, each item is a placeholder. If there is more than one placeholder, repeat the steps to highlight and replace each of them. After replacing all of them, press **Enter**, and the calculation is done! ■

Entering Text

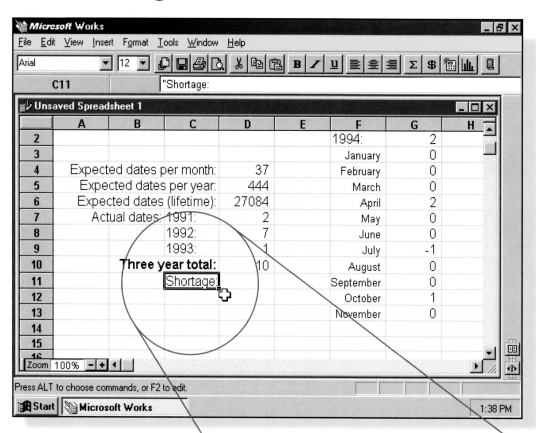

"Why would I do this?"

Without text, a spreadsheet would just be a huge grid of numbers. You might be able to keep track of what each of the numbers stands for, but it would be impossible for anyone else to tell. You can use text as labels for the different numbers and equations. For example, you might put "interest rate" next to the cell that contains the interest rate, or "January" over the column where you list your January bills, or "Total sales" next to the equation where you add it all up.

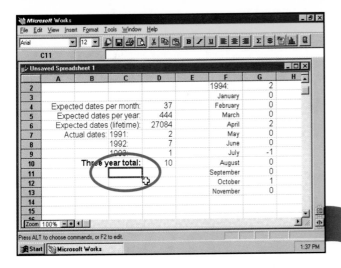

1 Select the cell into which you want to enter the text.

NOTE ▼

You can't put text in a cell with a number or an equation. You have to put it in the cell next to it.

2 Start typing, and the outline around the cell becomes thin. Keep your text short so it won't overlap something in another cell. What you type appears in the cell and on the editing line.

NOTE ▼

You can select any font and use the bold, italic, underline, and alignment buttons on the toolbar just as you do in the Works word processor.

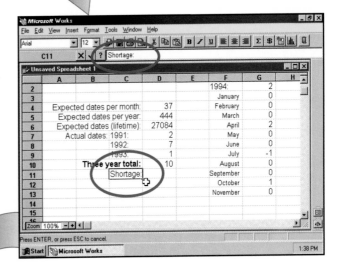

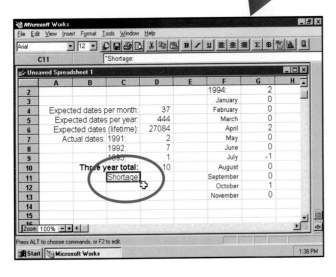

3 Press the **Enter** key. The outline around the cell becomes thick again, and Works enters the text in the cell. Quotation marks (") now appear before the text entry on the editing line. ■

WHY WORRY?

If the text isn't right, just double-click on the cell to select the text for editing.

TASK 39
Copying Cells

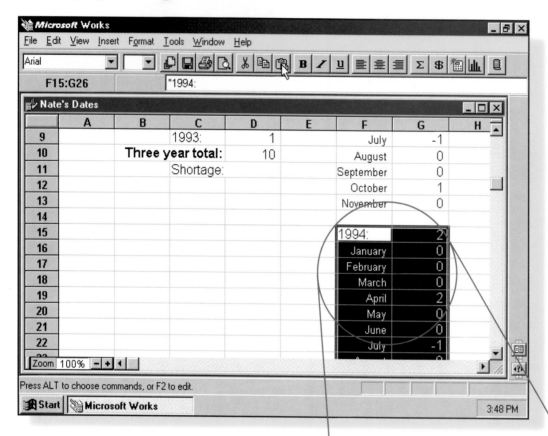

"Why would I do this?"

Sometimes you want certain numbers or equations to appear in more than one place in your spreadsheet. Works lets you copy cells from one place to another. This saves you a lot of retyping time.

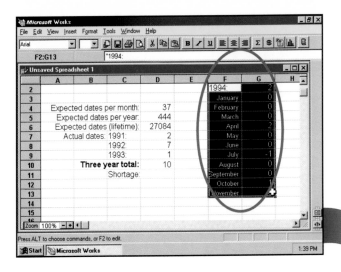

1 Select the range of cells you want to copy by dragging the mouse from one corner of the range to its diagonally opposite corner.

NOTE ▼

You can copy just one cell if you want to. Think of it as a small range of cells that's only one cell wide and one cell high.

2 Click on the **Copy** button on the toolbar.

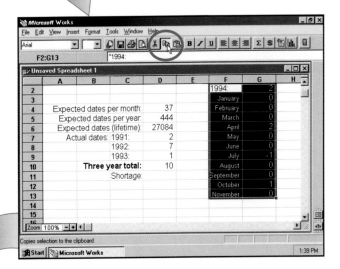

3 Select the cell in the upper-left corner of the range of cells you want to copy to.

NOTE ▼

Be careful! If there is data in any of the cells in the range you are copying to, that data will be replaced with what you copy.

4 Click on the **Paste** toolbar button, and Works places the copied cells in the new location. The copied cells remain selected.

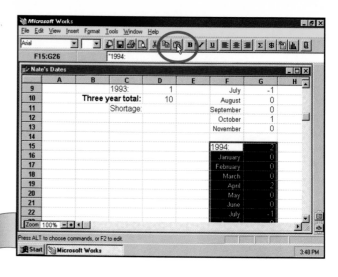

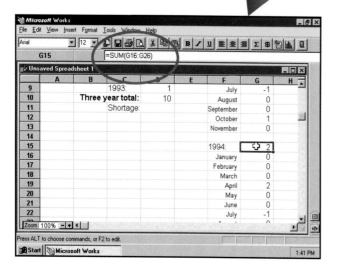

5 When you copy an equation with cell addresses in it, the addresses change to reflect the new location. For example, if you have the equation =3+E6 in cell D5, and you copy that to cell J8, the equation becomes =3+K9, which still refers to the data one cell down and one cell over from the equation. Therefore, the copied cells refer to the copied data instead of the original data. ■

NOTE ▼

If you make a mistake copying, just pull down the Edit menu and select the Undo Paste command. The copied data disappears, and any data that was there before the copy reappears!

Erasing Cells

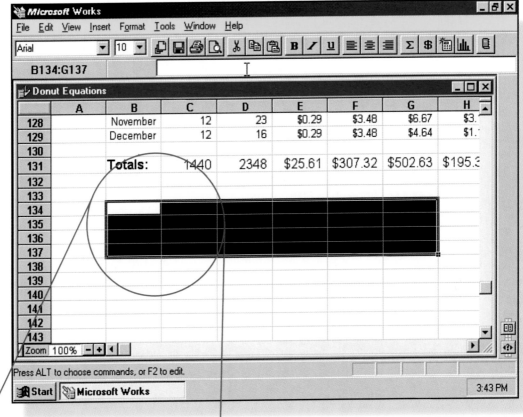

"Why would I do this?"

You aren't likely to fill up all the space on a spreadsheet. (After all, the spreadsheet has about 4 million cells!) However, when your spreadsheet is full of things you don't need any more, it's harder to find the things that you do need. A crowded spreadsheet slows down calculations when you add or change data. Plus, if you're going to show that budget to your boss or your client, you want it to look nice and neat!

1 Select the cell or cells you want to erase.

NOTE ▼

Be careful not to erase numbers that other calculations are based on. If you do, the answers to those calculations will change because Works will consider the erased value a zero.

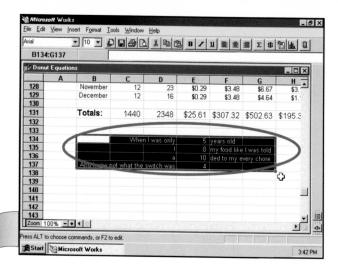

2 Click on the **Cut** button.

NOTE ▼

Hitting the Delete key produces the same effect.

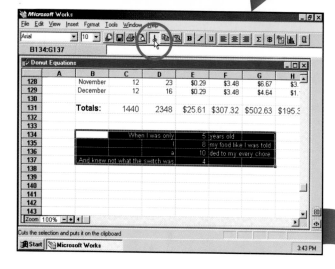

3 Works wipes out the entries in the selected cells, leaving them blank. ■

WHY WORRY?

If you accidentally erase the wrong cells, pull down the Edit menu and select the Undo Cut or Undo Clear command.

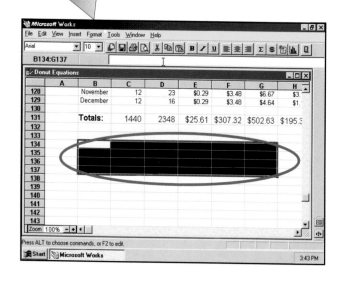

Showing Dollars and Cents

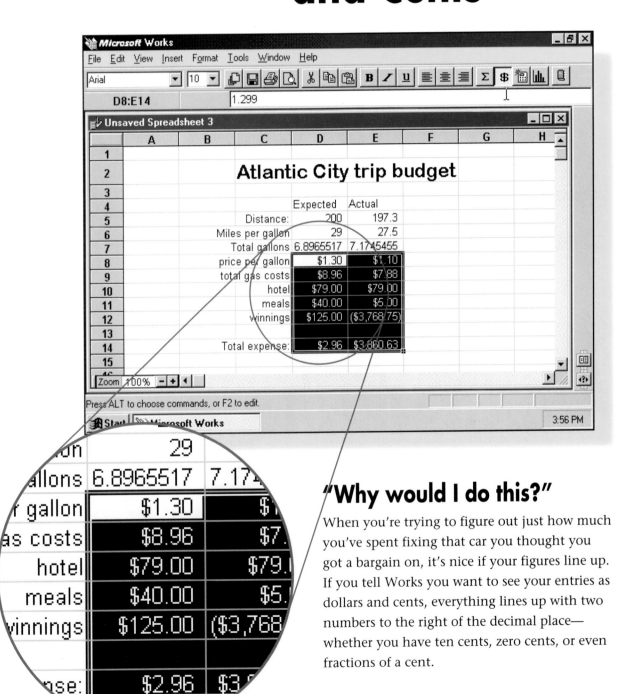

"Why would I do this?"

When you're trying to figure out just how much you've spent fixing that car you thought you got a bargain on, it's nice if your figures line up. If you tell Works you want to see your entries as dollars and cents, everything lines up with two numbers to the right of the decimal place—whether you have ten cents, zero cents, or even fractions of a cent.

1 Select the cell or cells you want to see as dollars and cents.

> Don't worry if your cell range has some text in it. This procedure won't change text at all.

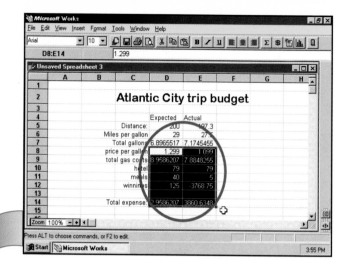

2 Click on the **Currency** button. It appears to be pressed in.

3 The numbers now appear as dollars and cents. Negative numbers have parentheses around them, as in ($327.05). Large numbers have commas after the thousands and the millions places, as in $7,001,327.05. ■

> If you decide you don't want the cells to show dollars and cents, select the cells again. The Currency button should still appear to be pressed in. Click on the Currency button again. It pops right out, and your numbers are back to normal!

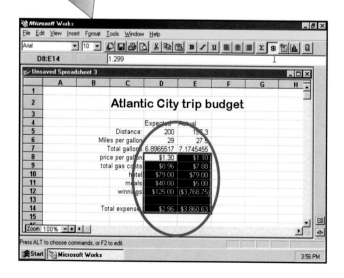

Creating a Graph

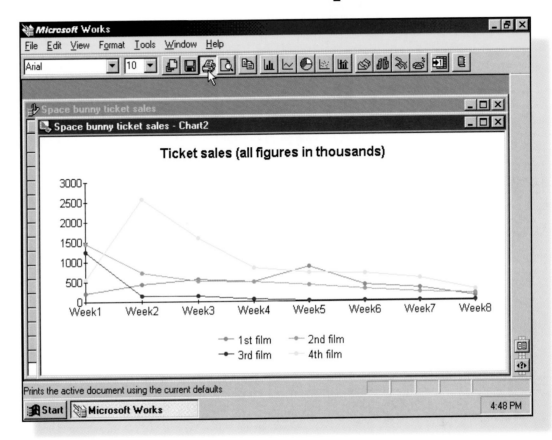

"Why would I do this?"

A graph is a good way of displaying numerical information so that people can get a quick sense of how different numbers relate to each other. Pie graphs show how a total breaks down into a few different parts. Bar graphs are good for comparing values or amounts of different things. Line graphs are good for showing change over time.

1 In a row of cells, enter the names of the different items you want to track with your graph. For example, if you are tracking sales, you might enter the products that you are tracking sales of. Leave a blank column to the left of this row of cells, and put only one name in each cell.

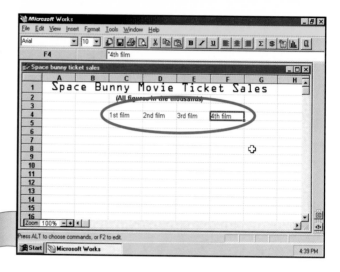

2 In the column you left blank, enter the names of the points that you are graphing for each of the items. For example, if you are tracking product sales by week, this would be a list of weeks. Start this list in the row below the row of names, and enter only one name in each cell.

3 Put in the numbers that you want to graph. Make sure each number is in the correct cell (at the intersection of the item column and data point row).

> **NOTE** ▼
>
> You can use equations in these cells. The graph will show the result of the equations.

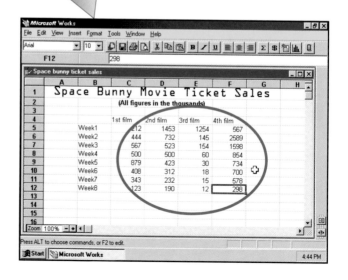

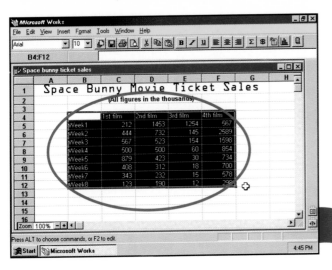

4 Select the range to be graphed, including the row and column with the names.

5 Click on the **New Chart** button.

NOTE ▼

Works refers to graphs as *charts*.

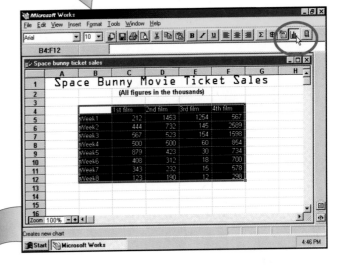

6 If this box comes up, click on the **OK** button to continue.

NOTE ▼

To have Works show you some things about making graphs, click on `Quick tour of charting.` To skip over this screen in the future, click the "Don't display this message in the future" check box.

7 The New Chart dialog box appears. Click on the picture of the graph type you want to create. The picture becomes highlighted with a dark gray background, and Works displays a sample of that graph with your data on the right side of the box.

> **NOTE** ▼
>
> Remember that pie graphs can only display information from one column of numbers.

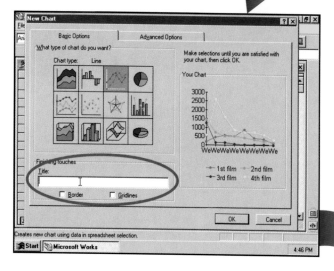

8 Click in the **Title** text box, and a blinking cursor line appears there.

9 Type a title for the graph. As you type, Works displays this title over the sample picture of your graph.

> **NOTE** ▼
>
> You can edit the name using the left and right arrow keys and the Backspace key.

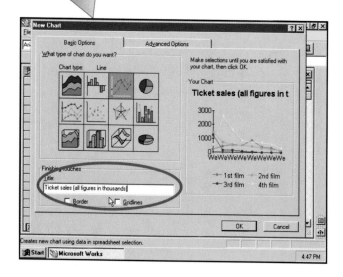

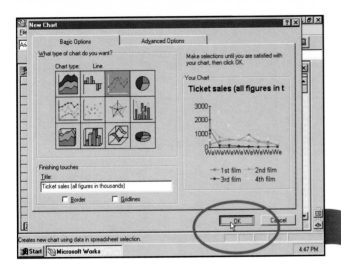

10 When you're satisfied with the graph shown in the sample, click on the **OK** button.

11 Works displays your graph in its own window. If you want to print the graph, just click on the **Print** button.

WHY WORRY?

All the information you typed in is still on the spreadsheet. If you're not happy with how the graph came out, select the range, click the Graph button again, and start over.

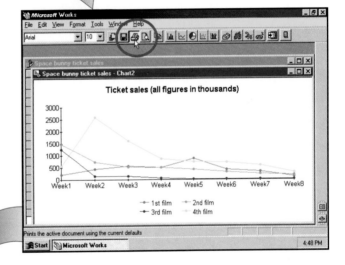

12 When you're done with the graph, pull down the **File** menu and select the **Close** command. The graph disappears, and you can go back to working with the spreadsheet. ■

Printing Your Spreadsheet

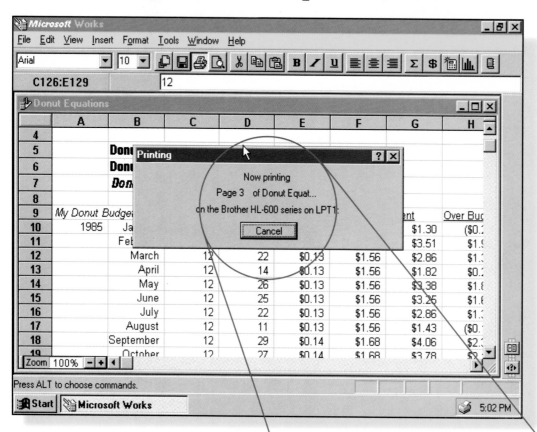

"Why would I do this?"

Sometimes you will need to give or mail your spreadsheet to someone else. That's when printing comes in handy. Printing your spreadsheet on paper and carrying the paper around is certainly a lot easier than lugging your computer!

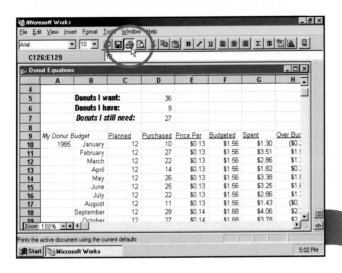

1 Click on the **Print** button.

NOTE ▼

Each printed page holds the section of a spreadsheet that's visible in a little more than one screen across and three screens down. If your spreadsheet is larger than that, it will print on multiple pages.

2 Works displays a dialog box that says Now printing. This dialog box also tells you which page Works is currently sending to the printer and which printer it's using.

WHY WORRY?

If you change your mind after Works starts printing your spreadsheet, just click on the Cancel button!

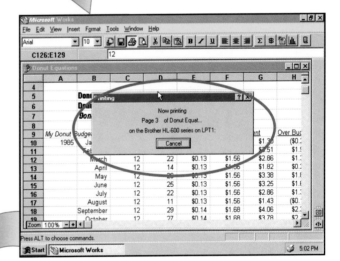

3 When Works finishes sending the document to the printer, the dialog box disappears, and you can continue working on your document. ■

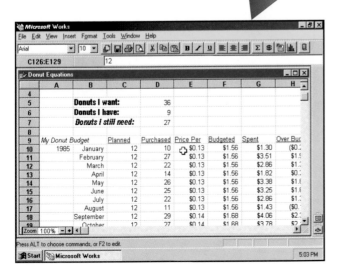

Saving Your Spreadsheet

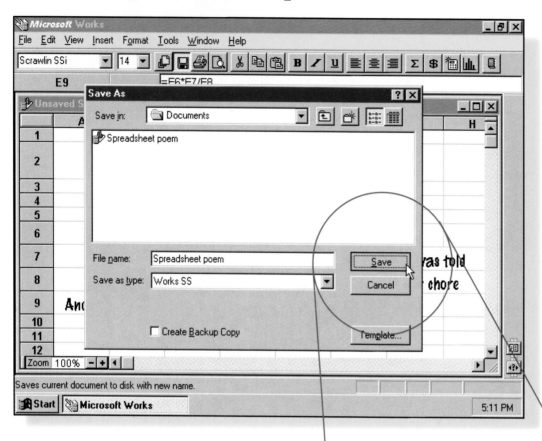

"Why would I do this?"

When you save a spreadsheet, Works puts a copy of it on your computer's disk so you can get it back again any time you want and look at it, change it, or print it. If you don't save your spreadsheet when you leave the program, the spreadsheet disappears forever. It's also a good idea to save your spreadsheet every few minutes while you're working on it, so that if something goes wrong, you won't lose all your work.

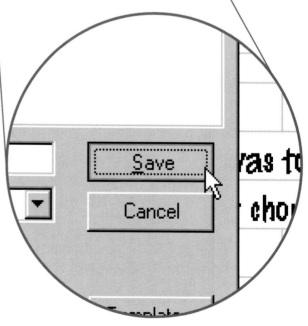

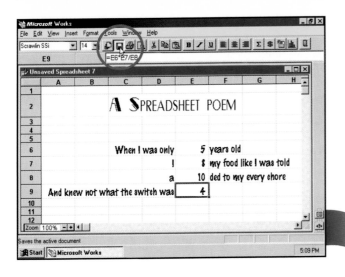

1 Click on the **Save** button. If you retrieved this spreadsheet or have previously saved it, Works replaces the copy already on the disk with this updated one, and you can continue working with your spreadsheet.

NOTE ▼

To keep the old copy, pull down the File menu and select the Save As command. Then continue with these instructions, giving the spreadsheet a new and different name.

2 If you have not saved this spreadsheet before, the Save As dialog box appears. Click in the File name text box and type in a name for the spreadsheet. Be sure to use a name that you can recognize and that it is different from the name of any other spreadsheet.

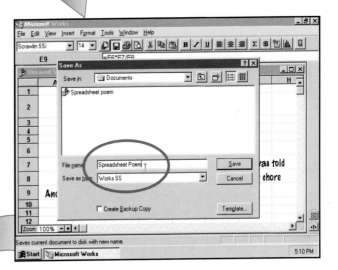

3 Click on the **Save** button at the bottom of the dialog box. Works saves the spreadsheet on the disk.

WHY WORRY?

If you decide that you don't want to save this file right now, click on the Cancel button and continue working on your spreadsheet.

4 If Works tells you The filename already exists, you've already used that name for another spreadsheet. Click on the **No** button.

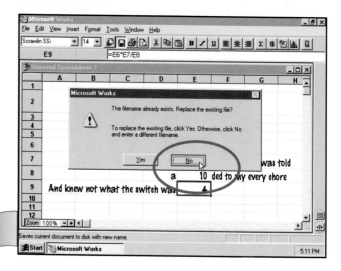

5 The Save As dialog box appears again. Type in a different name and click on the **Save** button.

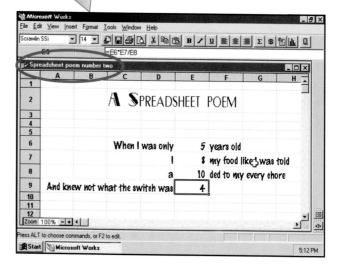

6 After you save the spreadsheet on the disk, you can continue working with it. At the top, Works displays the name you gave the spreadsheet. ■

Leaving the Spreadsheet

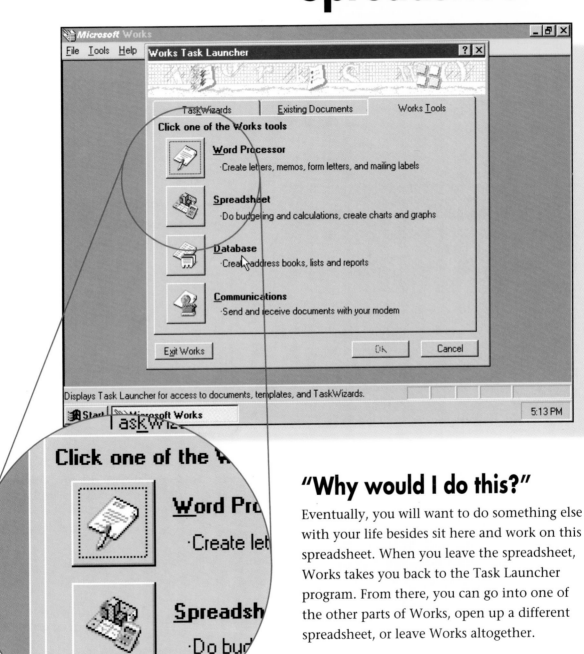

"Why would I do this?"

Eventually, you will want to do something else with your life besides sit here and work on this spreadsheet. When you leave the spreadsheet, Works takes you back to the Task Launcher program. From there, you can go into one of the other parts of Works, open up a different spreadsheet, or leave Works altogether.

1 Pull down the **File** menu and select the **Close** command.

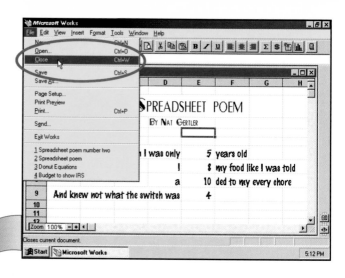

NOTE ▼

There are two shortcuts for doing this: hold down Ctrl and press W, or click on the X button above the upper-right corner of the spreadsheet.

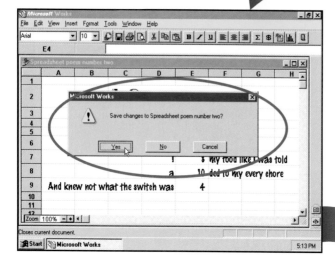

2 If you have made changes to the file since the last time you saved it, clicking **Yes** as if you used the Save command.

NOTE ▼

If you loaded this document from disk or have saved it before, and you want to save it under a different name, you have to hit the Cancel button and use the Save As command to save the file with a different name. Then you can leave the program.

3 The Task Launcher screen appears. ■

WHY WORRY?

If after saving and leaving your spreadsheet you decide that you aren't done working with it, you can load it again and get back to work on it!

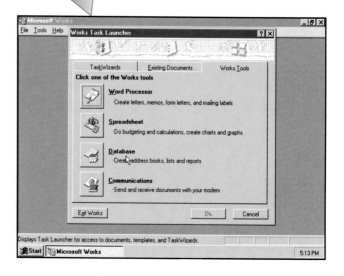

Copying Cells to a Word Processor Document

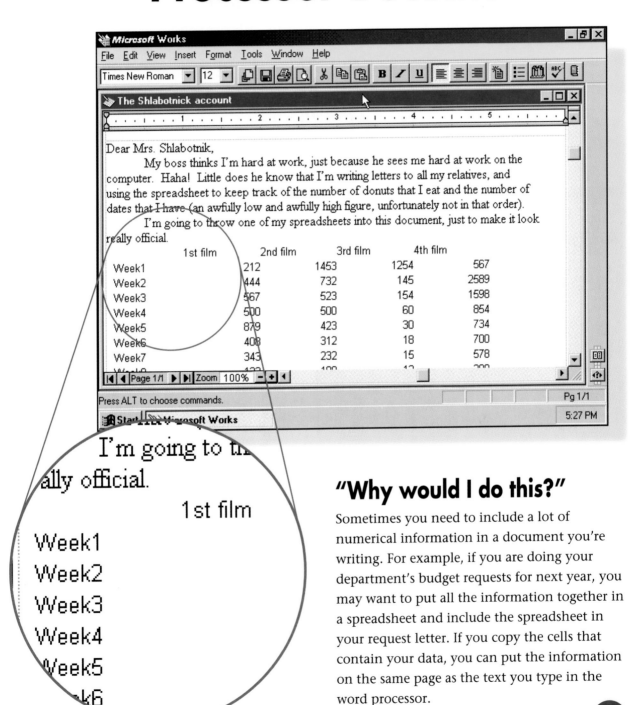

"Why would I do this?"

Sometimes you need to include a lot of numerical information in a document you're writing. For example, if you are doing your department's budget requests for next year, you may want to put all the information together in a spreadsheet and include the spreadsheet in your request letter. If you copy the cells that contain your data, you can put the information on the same page as the text you type in the word processor.

1 In the spreadsheet, select the cells you want to copy.

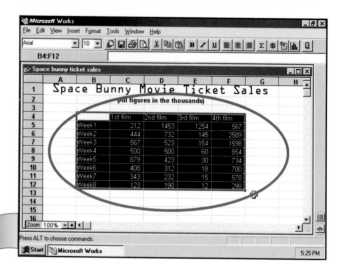

2 Click on the **Copy** button.

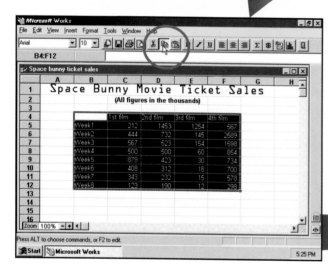

3 If you've made any changes to the spreadsheet that you want to save, click on the **Save** button.

> **NOTE** ▼
>
> Remember, you can save the file under a different name by pulling down the File menu, selecting the Save As command, and entering the new name in the Save As dialog box.

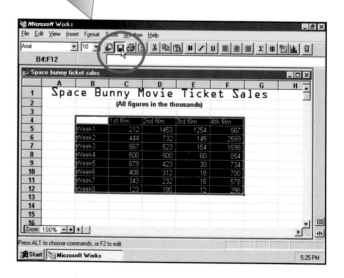

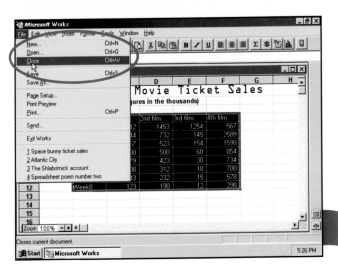

4 Pull down the **File** menu and select the **Close** command to leave the spreadsheet program.

5 Using the Task Launcher, open up the word processing document that you want to put the cells in. Select the name of the document and click **OK**.

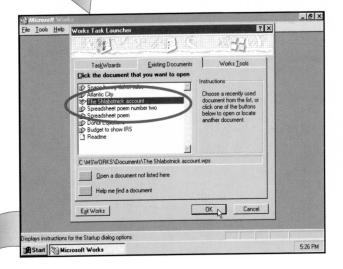

6 Put the cursor at the start of a blank line where you want to place the spreadsheet data.

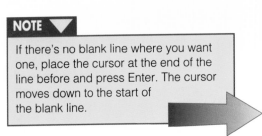

NOTE ▼

If there's no blank line where you want one, place the cursor at the end of the line before and press Enter. The cursor moves down to the start of the blank line.

7 Click on the **Paste** button.

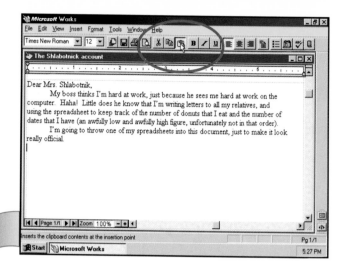

8 The spreadsheet data appears in the word processor document. Works doesn't display any equations or the gridlines, just labels and numbers. If any of the cells originally contained equations, you now see the results of the calculations. ■

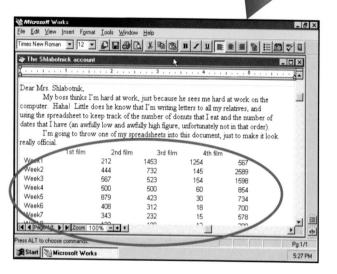

WHY WORRY?

If you don't like where you put the cells, just pull down the Edit menu and select the Undo Paste command. The cells disappear. Repeat steps 6 through 8 to put them where you want.

PART IV

Using the Communications Program

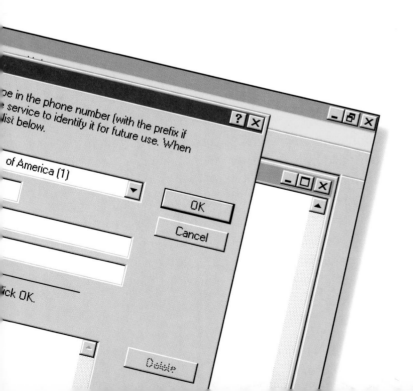

Your computer can contact other computers via telephone lines. Using the communications program, you can take advantage of special services that the other computer provides. These days, those special services include everything from booking your plane reservations to sending a note to a friend.

In order for your computer to use the phone lines, it has to be attached to a device called a *modem*. Some modems, called internal modems, are installed inside your computer; others, called external modems, are small boxes that are attached to your computer by a cable. The modem translates the information your computer gives it into a language that sounds to humans like high-pitched whistles and other noise. The computer on the other end of the line also has a modem, which hears the whistles and translates them back into computer information. By translating, sending, and receiving these sounds over telephone wires, your modem makes it possible for you to send and receive information and communicate with other computers.

When you use the communications program in Works, whatever you type is sent out to the other computer. You can use the communications program to contact computer services (often called *online services*) where you can read messages from other people, type messages to other people, look up information, play games, check out the latest news, order things from a computerized catalog, or do literally thousands of other different things.

Just as your computer is running Works communications program, the other computer is running a program that tells it how to interpret and react to what you type. There are many different types of programs available, and each works a bit differently. Because of this, there's no way we can tell you how the program on the other computer works. However, we can (and do!) tell you how to get that other program started.

The people who design communications programs realize that many users won't know how to use them, so they make the programs tell you what to do. It might ask you for specific information such as your name. Just type in what it asks for, and then hit the **Enter** key. If it gives you a list of things that you can do with a letter next to each one, press the key of the letter next to what you want to do. Wait a second, and if nothing happens, hit the **Enter** key. If you don't know what the computer wants, type help and press **Enter**. Often the other computer will give you a helpful response.

There are many useful and fun things you can do with online computer services. Although you must pay to use some services, you can use others (usually smaller, local ones) for only the cost of the phone call. There are services out there for everyone. The most important thing is that you start exploring now. The more you reach out to other computers and use their programs, the easier it becomes.

The Works communications program will not work with some of the larger computer services. This is because services such as PRODIGY, America Online, and The Microsoft Network use a lot of graphics to interact with you, and a normal communications program can only understand and display simple text. In order to use one of those services, you need a program designed just for that service. These services usually find ways to give the programs away for free, to encourage people to try the service.

The software for The Microsoft Network comes free with the Windows 95 operating system. If you want to learn how to use this software, read my next book, *Easy Microsoft Network*, available in better book stores in December 1995.

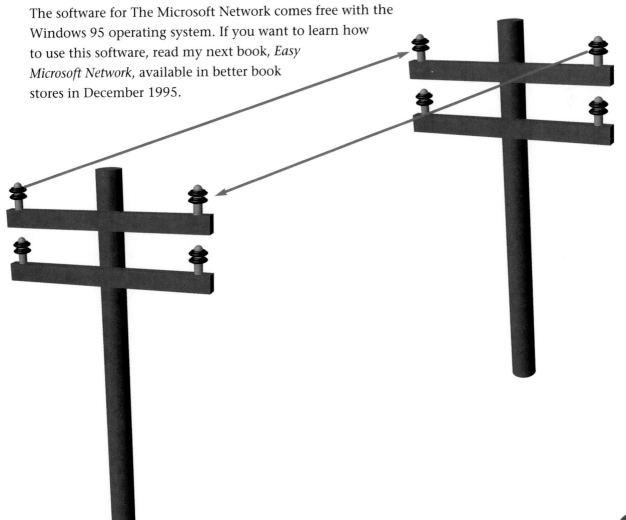

Starting the Communications Program

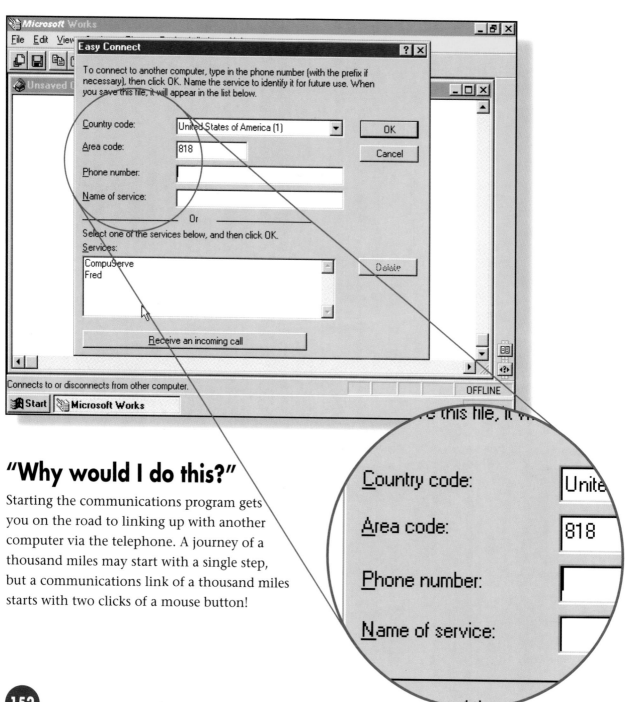

"Why would I do this?"

Starting the communications program gets you on the road to linking up with another computer via the telephone. A journey of a thousand miles may start with a single step, but a communications link of a thousand miles starts with two clicks of a mouse button!

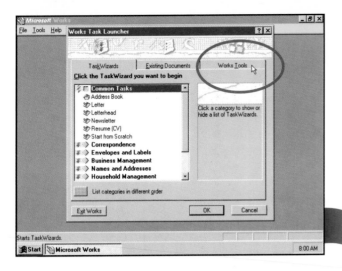

1 On the Task Launcher screen, click on the **Works Tools** tab. Works displays a set of four buttons, one for each of the main programs it provides.

2 Click on the **Communications** button.

WHY WORRY?

If you don't want to use the communications program, click on the Cancel button to get rid of the Easy Connect dialog box. Then pull down the File menu and select the Close command, and you're back at the Task Launcher screen.

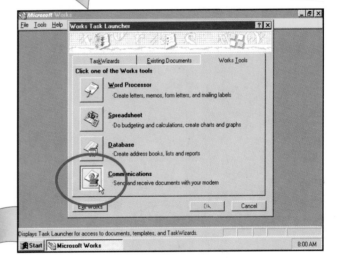

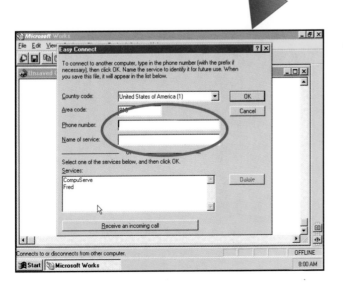

3 Works starts the communications program and automatically displays the Easy Connect dialog box so you can tell it which number to dial. Behind the dialog box is the main communications program screen. ■

TASK 48
Calling a New Service

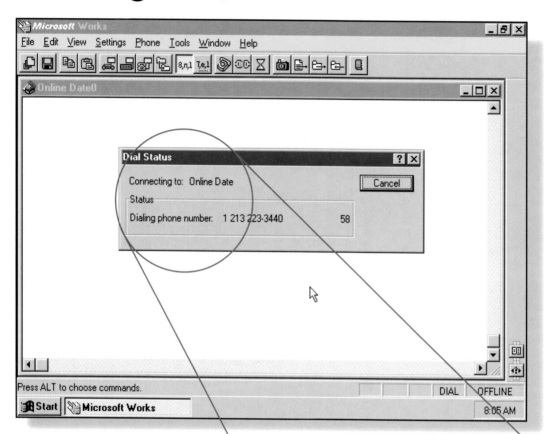

"Why would I do this?"

For your computer to reach another computer by phone, it has to call that computer's modem. When you find out about a service that you want to call, be sure to ask for the phone number, because these numbers are often not listed in the phone book. Then you need to tell your computer that number so it can start dialing.

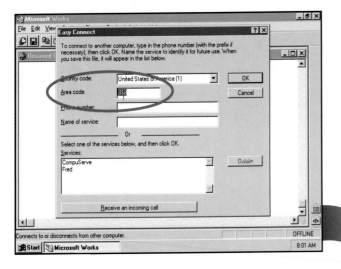

1 Double-click on the number in the **Area code** text box. This causes the number's background to turn blue, which indicates it's selected.

> **NOTE** ▼
>
> If the area code of the phone number you want to dial is the one displayed, you can skip steps 1 and 2.

2 Type the area code of the phone number you want the computer to dial. The old number disappears, and the new number takes its place in the box.

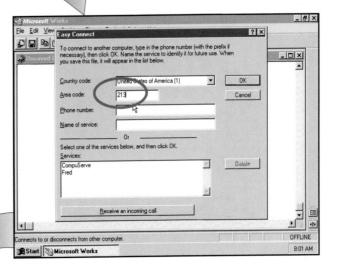

3 Click on the **Phone number** text box, and the blinking cursor appears there.

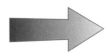

4 Enter the rest of the phone number you want to call.

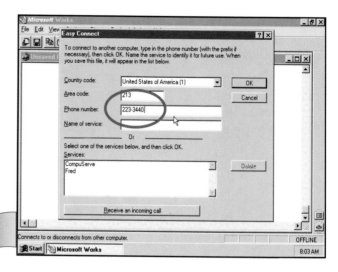

5 Click in the **Name of service** text box, and the blinking cursor moves to that box.

6 Type the name of the service whose phone number you entered. Make sure it's a name that you'll recognize when you want to call this service again.

NOTE ▼

If you're never going to call this number again, you can skip step 6.

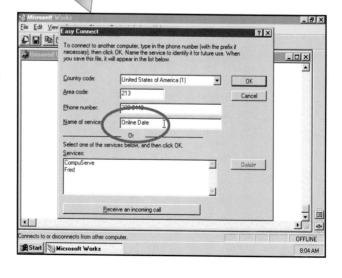

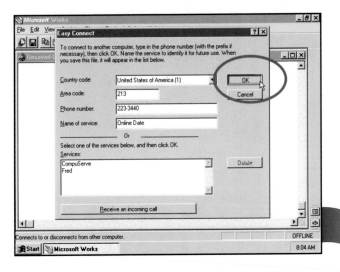

7 When you have entered everything correctly, click on the **OK** button. The Easy Connect dialog box disappears.

8 In the Dial dialog box, verify the phone number you want to dial and click on the **Dial** button.

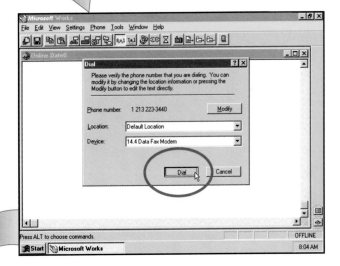

9 Works displays the Dial Status dialog box while your computer dials the other computer and makes certain they are communicating clearly.

10 When they are, the Dial Status dialog box disappears and you should see a blank white screen. The Dial/Hangup toolbar button should appear to be pressed.

WHY WORRY?

If the Dial/Hangup button is not pressed, the computers did not connect. The phone line might be busy, or it might have been a bad connection. Click the Dial/Hangup button to try again.

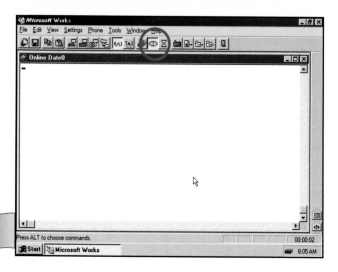

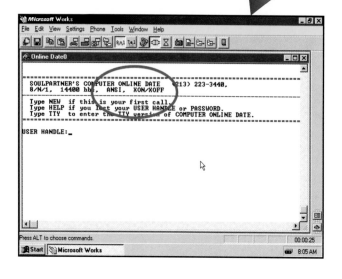

11 If the Dial/Hangup button is pressed but the other computer doesn't send some information to your screen within a few seconds, try pressing **Enter** a couple of times. ■

WHY WORRY?

You can stop the dialing process by clicking on the Cancel button in the Easy Connect dialog box, the Dial dialog box, or the Dial Status dialog box.

Calling a Service You've Called Before

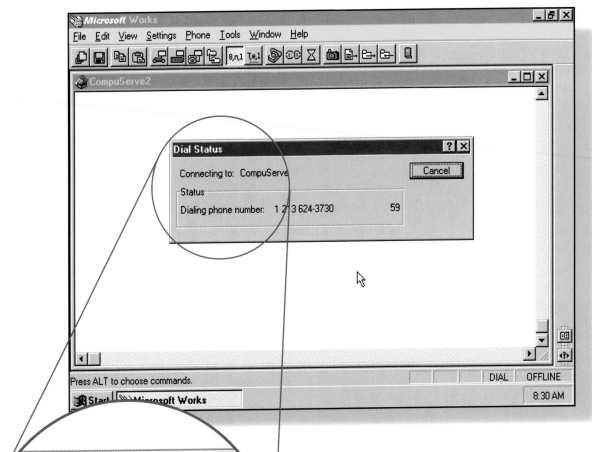

"Why would I do this?"

Once you've called a service and stored its phone number and information, you never have to enter the phone number again. The computer keeps a phone book with that information in it. You simply pick the name of the system you want to call, and the computer dials it up.

1 In the Easy Connect dialog box, click on the name of the system you want to call. The name becomes highlighted.

The entries in the Services list are in alphabetical order. You may need to use the scroll bars to find the system you want.

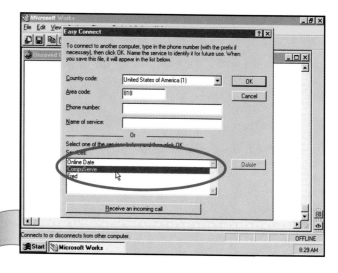

2 Click on the **OK** button, and the Easy Connect dialog box disappears.

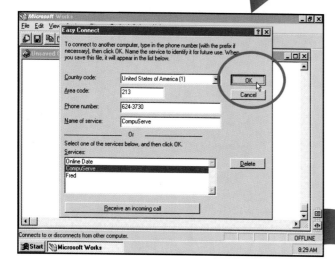

3 In the Dial dialog box, verify the phone number and click on the **Dial** button.

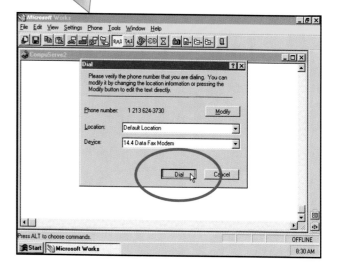

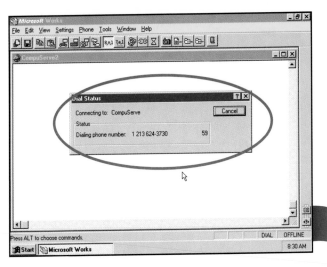

4 Works displays the Dial Status dialog box while your computer dials up the other computer and makes certain that they are communicating clearly.

5 When Works knows the computers are communicating clearly, the Dial Status dialog box disappears. You should see a blank white screen, and the Dial/Hangup toolbar button should appear to be pressed.

If the Dial/Hangup button is not pressed, the computers did not connect. The phone line might be busy, or it might have been a bad connection. Click the **Dial/Hangup** button to try again.

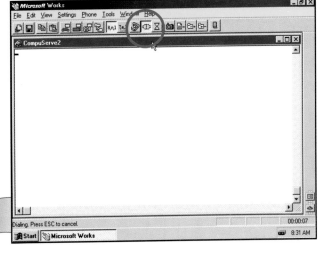

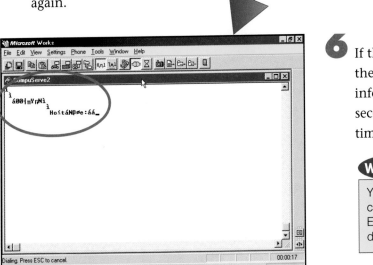

6 If the Dial/Hangup button is pressed but the other computer doesn't send some information to your screen within a few seconds, try hitting **Enter** a couple of times. ∎

WHY WORRY?

You can stop the dialing process by clicking on the Cancel button in the Easy Connect dialog box, the Dial dialog box, or the Dial Status dialog box.

Changing the Settings

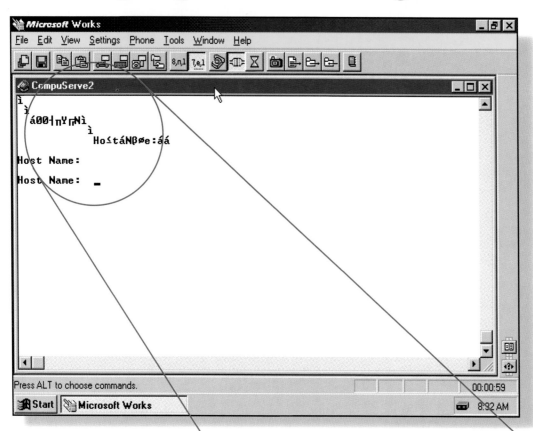

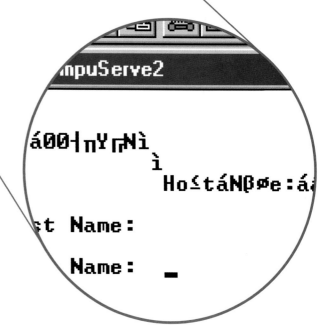

"Why would I do this?"

Computers have several different codes they can use to talk between themselves. If your computer isn't using the same code as the other computer, your computer won't be able to understand what the other computer is saying. Luckily, most computer services use one of two main codes. Works makes it easy for you to switch between the settings for those codes.

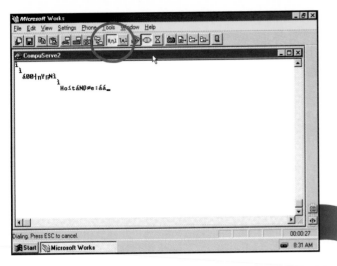

1 When you first dial a new number, Works automatically uses the 8,N,1 setting, and the 8,N,1 setting toolbar button is pressed. This is the best setting to use when trying a new number.

2 If what the other computer sends you appears to be gibberish, you're using the wrong setting. (About half the characters will appear to be normal letters, but the other half will be letters with accent marks, little shapes, and other odd things.) Click on the **7,E,1 setting** button on the toolbar.

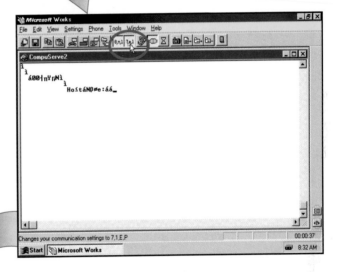

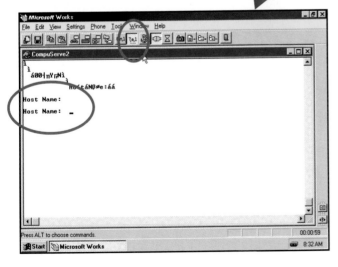

3 The 7,E,1 setting button now appears to be pressed, and the 8,N,1 setting button pops out. All the text from this point on should be readable. ■

WHY WORRY?

To switch the settings back, just click on the 8,N,1 setting button again.

Hanging Up

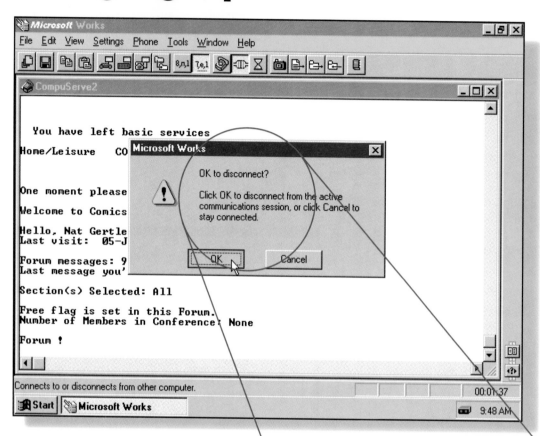

"Why would I do this?"

When people finish talking on the phone, they hang up. Likewise, when your computer finishes talking to another computer over the phone lines, it needs to hang up. Sometimes the computer on the other end hangs up first, in which case your computer hangs up automatically. However, when the other computer doesn't hang up first, you have to tell your computer to hang up.

OK to disconnect?

Click OK to disconnect from the communications session, or click stay connected.

1 Check the Dial/Hangup button to see if the other computer has already hung up. If the button is pressed, the other computer has not hung up, and you have to do it.

2 To hang up, click once on the **Dial/Hangup** button. The button appears to pop out, and the cables shown on it become disconnected.

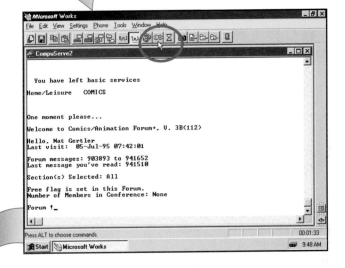

3 Works then double-checks by asking you if it's OK to disconnect? Click on the **OK** button, and your computer hangs up. ■

WHY WORRY?

If you accidentally click the Dial/Hangup button after your computer has already hung up, the program tries to dial the number again. Click the Cancel button in the Dial Status dialog box to stop it.

165

Leaving the Communications Program

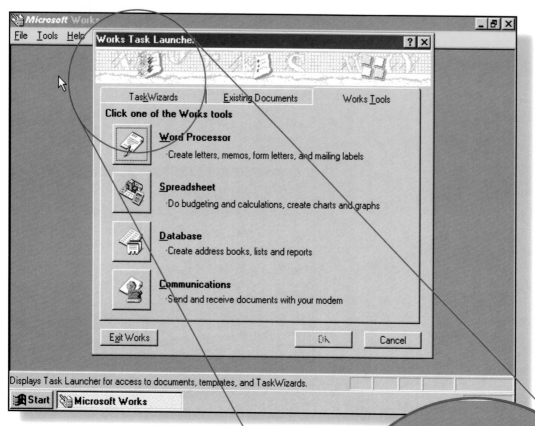

"Why would I do this?"

When you finish using another computer or service and you've hung up, you can leave the communications program and move on to other work.

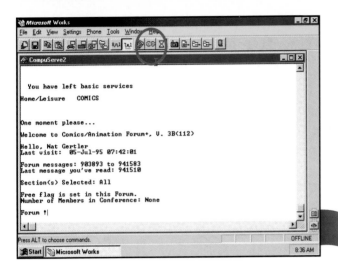

1 Make sure the Dial/Hangup button is not pressed. (If it is, you have to hang up the line by clicking on the **Dial/Hangup** button and clicking **OK** in the resulting dialog box.)

2 Pull down the **File** menu and select the **Close** command.

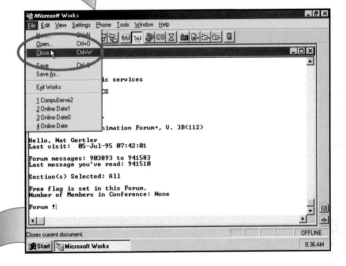

3 Works exits the communications program and returns you to the Task Launcher. ■

PART V

Using the Database Program

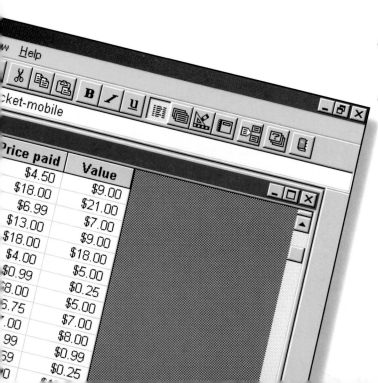

A *database* is just a computerized list. Suppose, for example, you have a list of the comic books in your comic book collection. For each comic book, you keep track of the title, the issue number, the names of the writer and artist, the condition the comic is in, and how much you paid for it. If you're more business-minded, suppose you have a list of clients that includes their names, phone numbers, the amounts of money they owe, and their credit limits.

In a database, each item you're keeping track of (each comic book or each client, for example) is a *record*. Each piece of information you're keeping track of (title, issue number, phone number, credit limit, and so on) is a *field*.

By keeping this list in a database, you can do things that you couldn't do easily if you kept a handwritten list or even a list in a word processor. The database program can pick out certain records based on guidelines that you set and print a list of those sorted items based on other guidelines. For example, you could print a list of your comic books, with the ones that you paid the least for at the top and the ones that you paid the most for at the bottom. Or you could print a list of only those clients with credit limits over $5000, listed in order of how much they owe you.

The database program in Works can store thousands of records in a single database. The longer your list, the more important it is to keep it in a database. After all, it might be easy to look down a list of a hundred clients for those who are over their limits, but if you're keeping track of thousands of clients, it's much easier to let the computer do it.

Before you start a database, try to think of all the fields you are going to need. Although it is possible to add more fields after you create the database (in fact, Works makes doing so amazingly easy), if you already have records in your database, you will have to go back and figure out what goes into that field for all of the existing records. You should also know that it's best to sort and select whole fields. Because of this, if you want to be able to search for just the clients in a certain city, the street address and the city must be in separate fields instead of one big one. A little planning ahead of time can save you a lot of effort later.

This section gets you started using your database. However, there is much more that you can do with the database program. Once you're comfortable with the skills you learn here, use the Help system to learn more about making *reports* and using forms.

You can print reports that show only certain fields from the database, which means you get only the specific information you need. For example, if you have a database of your comic books, and each entry shows the title, the issue number, the names of the writers and artists, the condition of your copy, the characters that appear in the stories, the date the story was released, the cover price, the price you paid, and the comic's current value, you're looking at a lot of information. If you're going to the local comic book store to see if it has any issues of your favorite series that you don't have, you can print out just the titles and issue numbers of the ones you do have. That saves you a lot of paper and makes it much easier to look through.

Works also lets you design on-screen forms for entering and examining records. Because these forms show you an entire record at once as you enter it, it's easier to enter a record that's longer than one line of type. Again, the Help system has a wealth of information on this.

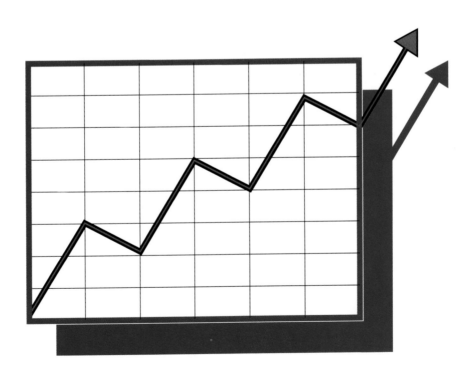

Creating a New Database

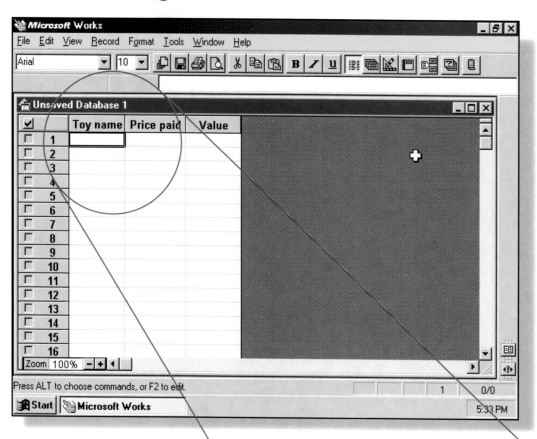

"Why would I do this?"

This is the first step to building your list. You need to tell the computer what the fields for the database are, so it knows what it has to keep track of.

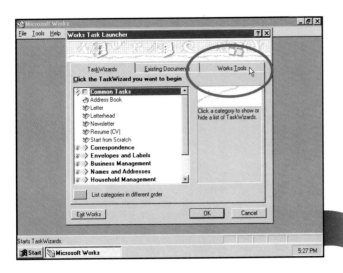

1 On the Task Launcher screen, click on the **Works Tools** tab. The Works Tools tab contains four buttons, one for each of the main programs in Works.

2 Click on the **Database** button.

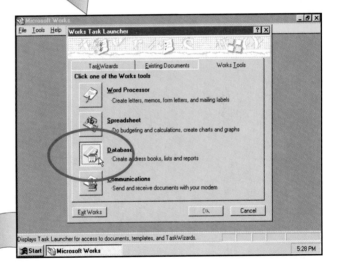

3 If Works displays this dialog box, click on the **OK** button to continue.

NOTE ▼

To have Works show you some things about making a database, click on the button next to `Quick tour of creating databases`. To skip over this screen in the future, click on the "Don't display this message in the future" check box.

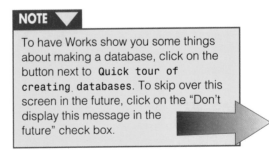

4 The Create Database dialog box appears and Field 1 is highlighted in blue in the Field name text box. This dialog box controls all the information for a single field.

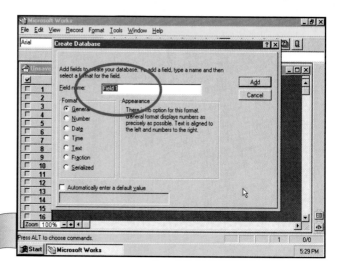

5 Type a name for the first field using no more than 15 characters. Pick a useful name because it will appear at the top of the field column to remind you what to put in the field. As you type, the name appears in the Field name text box.

6 Choose a field type from the Format list. Text format is good for names, addresses, and other things that aren't just numbers; Date format is good for dates; Number format is good for dollars and cents and other types of values you might use in calculations.

> **NOTE** ▼
>
> Phone numbers and ZIP codes should be stored in text format, not number format.

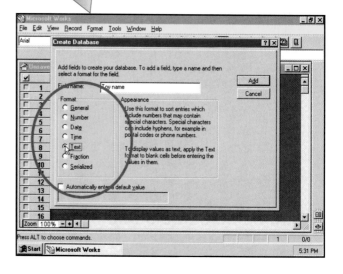

174

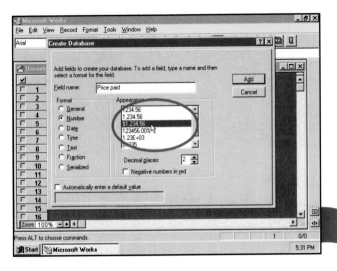

7 Depending on which format you choose, a list might appear in the Appearance box. If so, click on the style with which you want Works to display your information, and your selection becomes highlighted in blue.

> **NOTE** ▼
>
> Use the scroll bar to scroll through the list if necessary.

8 Click on the **Add** button to add this field to your new database.

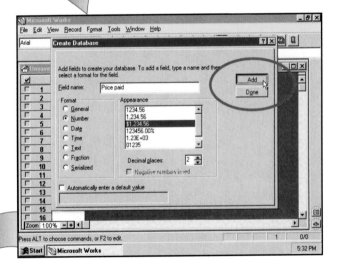

9 The Create Database dialog box displays Field 2 in the Field name text box so you can describe another field. Repeat steps 5 through 8 for each field you want in your database.

10

When you finish adding fields, click on the **Done** button.

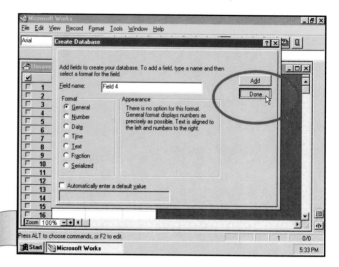

11

The dialog box disappears, and Works displays your database with the list of field names across the top. Later you will enter your records in the numbered rows below that. ■

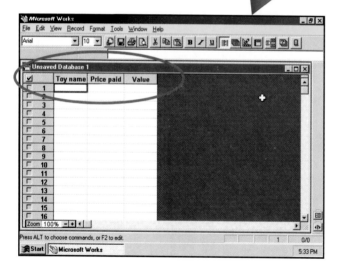

Using an Existing Database

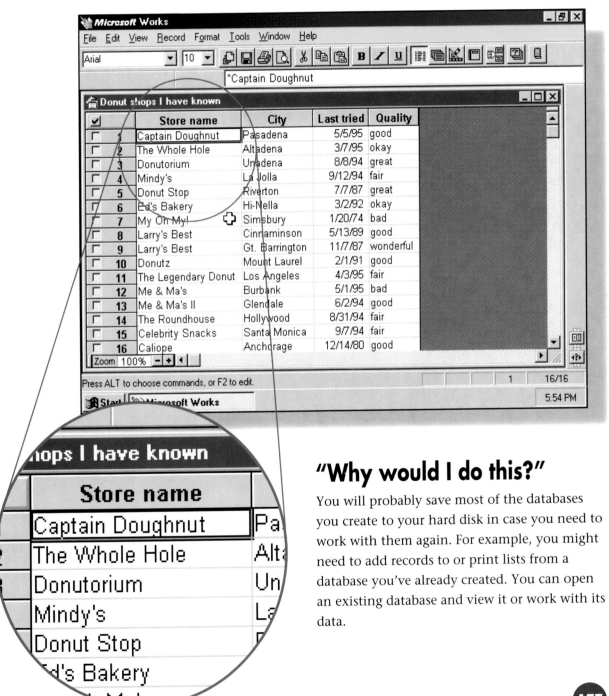

"Why would I do this?"

You will probably save most of the databases
you create to your hard disk in case you need to
work with them again. For example, you might
need to add records to or print lists from a
database you've already created. You can open
an existing database and view it or work with its
data.

1 On the Task Launcher screen, click the **Existing Documents** tab. Works displays a list of documents, spreadsheets, and databases you've worked with recently.

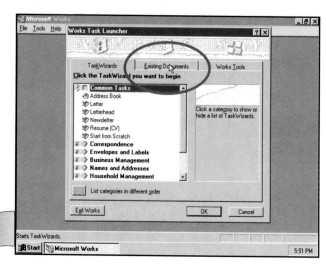

2 Scroll through the list if necessary and double-click on the name of the database you are looking for. (Each database has a picture of Rolodex cards next to its name.) Works starts the database program and displays the database you chose.

3 If you cannot find your database on that list, click on the **Open a document not listed here** button.

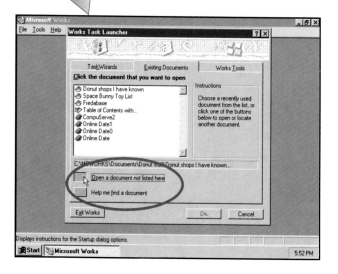

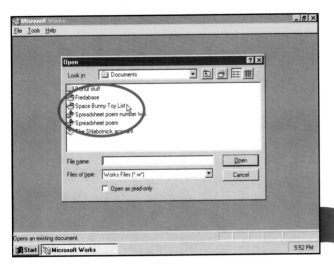

4 Works displays the **Open** dialog box, which contains a more complete list. If your database is listed there, -click on it.

5 If you stored the database in a folder, double-click on that folder, and the list of documents in that folder appears. Then double-click on the name of your database.

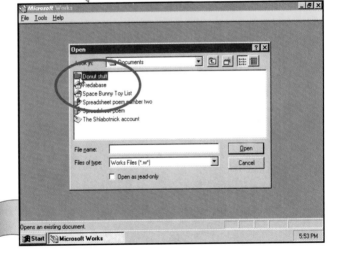

NOTE ▼

The Look in text box displays the name of the folder whose contents are currently displayed. If that's not the folder you want to look in, click on the button with the picture of a folder with an arrow on it. This brings you up out of that folder.

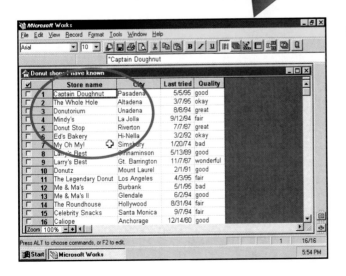

6 When you select your database file, Works starts the database program and displays your selected database. ■

WHY WORRY?

If you open the wrong database, pull down the File menu and select the Close command. This doesn't mess up the database you opened, it just returns you to the Task Launcher so you can get the right one.

Making a Field Longer or Shorter

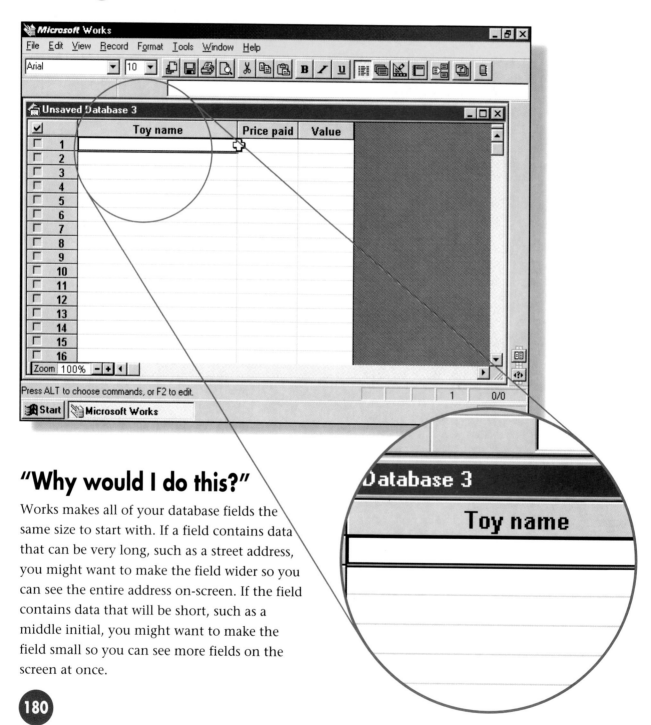

"Why would I do this?"

Works makes all of your database fields the same size to start with. If a field contains data that can be very long, such as a street address, you might want to make the field wider so you can see the entire address on-screen. If the field contains data that will be short, such as a middle initial, you might want to make the field small so you can see more fields on the screen at once.

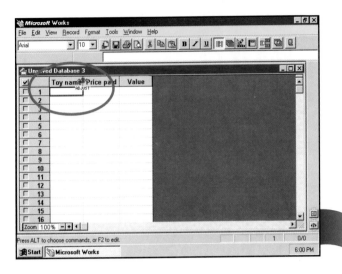

1 Position your pointer on the dividing line to the right of the field name. The pointer turns into a pair of arrows pointing left and right, with the word ADJUST below it.

NOTE ▼

To make the field just wide enough to hold the longest entry currently in that field, just double-click on the field name.

2 Press and hold the left mouse button and move the mouse. A dotted line appears to show you where the new edge of the field will be. To make the field larger, move it to the right. To make the field smaller, move it to the left.

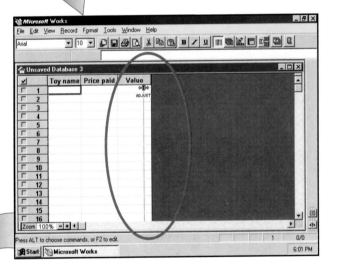

3 When the dotted line indicates the desired field size, let go of the mouse button. Works resizes that field and moves the others over to make room. ■

WHY WORRY?

If you changed the width of a field you didn't want to change or you didn't get the width right, pull down the Edit menu and select the Undo Field Width command.

Adding a New Record

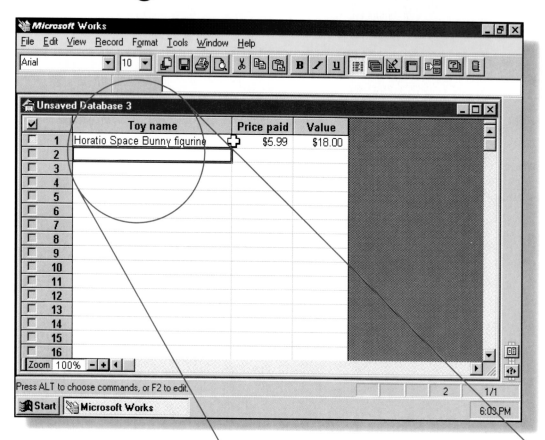

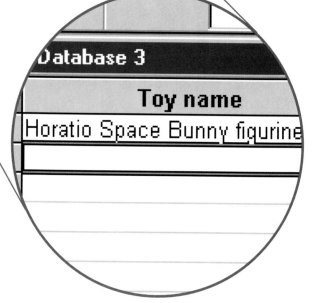

"Why would I do this?"

You'll want to add a new record to your database any time you have something new for your list. Each item on your list takes up one record.

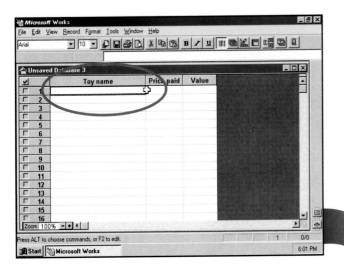

1 Click on the first field of the first blank row in your database. A thick black line surrounds it to indicate that it is active.

> **NOTE** ▼
>
> If you have a large database, there's a quicker way to get down to the first blank row. Press and hold Ctrl and hit the End key. Then let go of the Ctrl key and press Tab.

2 Type the entry for this field for this record.

> **NOTE** ▼
>
> You can use the Backspace key to correct typing mistakes.

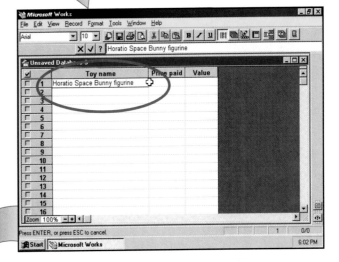

3 When you finish entering the data for that field, press **Tab** to move to the next field. The thick black line surrounds that field.

4 Repeat steps 2 and 3 for every field in the record.

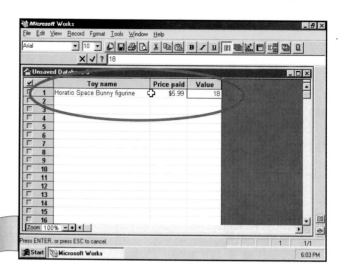

5 After you type the data in the last field, hit **Tab** once more. The thick black line moves to the first field of the next row so you can add another record. ■

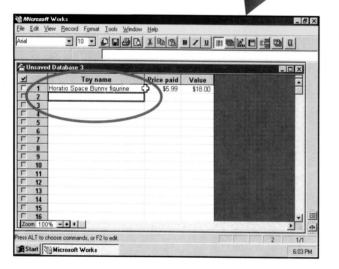

WHY WORRY?

If you make a mistake when entering a record, simply change or delete it.

Finding a Record

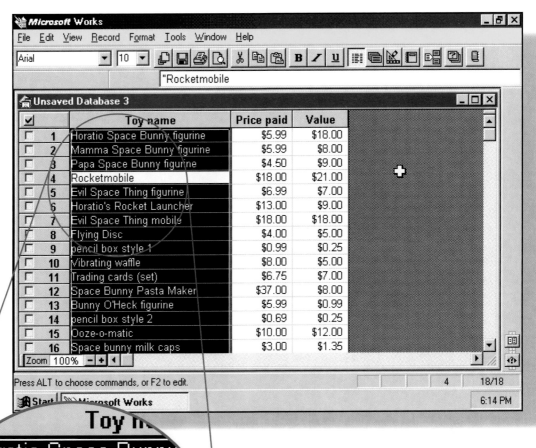

"Why would I do this?"

If you want to view, erase, or make changes to a record, you have to be able to locate it. In a short database, you can just look through the list to find it. However, if the list fills more than a couple of screens, it's quicker to let Works do the looking for you.

1 Click on the field name for the field you want to search in. When you do, Works displays a black border around the entire field, including all the records. The first record in the field has a white background, and the others have a black background.

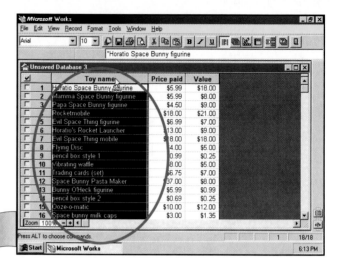

2 Pull down the **Edit** menu and select the **Find** command.

NOTE ▼

A shortcut for this is to hold down the Ctrl key and press F.

3 Type the information you are searching for in the Find what text box.

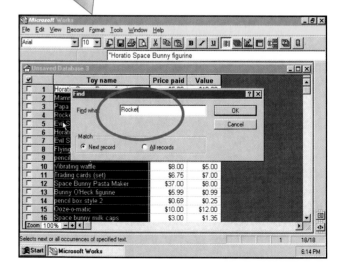

186

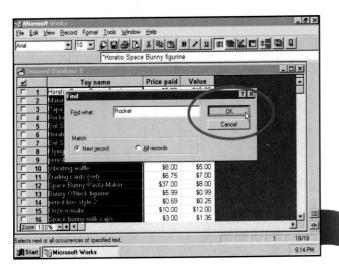

4 Click on the **OK** button to start the search.

> **NOTE** ▼
>
> Anytime you're told to click on the OK button, you can press Enter instead.

5 Works searches the field for the information you entered. When it finds a match, it displays the first matching record on a white background.

> **NOTE** ▼
>
> If this is not the record you're looking for, press and hold the Shift key and hit F4 to have Works search again.

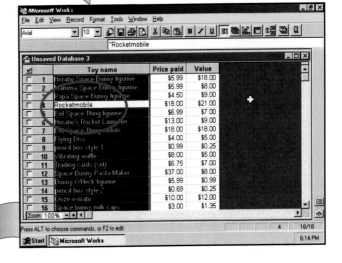

6 If no record contains the text you specified, Works tells you Works did not find a match. Click on the **OK** button to continue. ■

187

Changing a Record

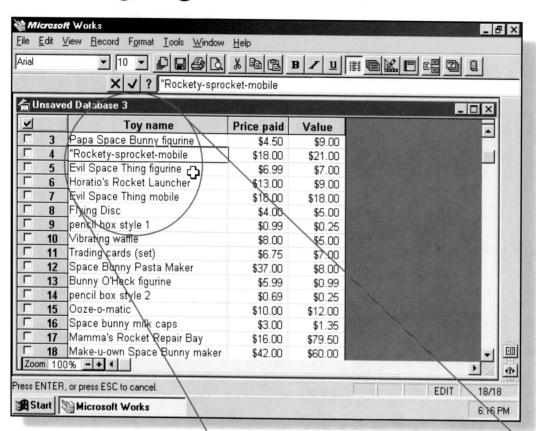

"Why would I do this?"

You might need to change a record if you made a mistake when you were entering it or if some of the information in the record changes. For example, if a client changes her address, you need to change the address fields in her record of your database.

1 Double-click on the item you want to change. Works displays a thin border around the item, and a blinking cursor line appears at the end of the text.

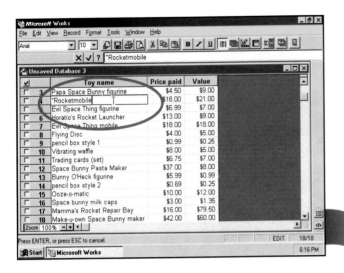

2 Change any necessary information in the record. Use the left and right cursor arrow keys to move through the text, and use the Backspace key (which may be marked "bkspc" or with an arrow pointing to the left) to erase characters.

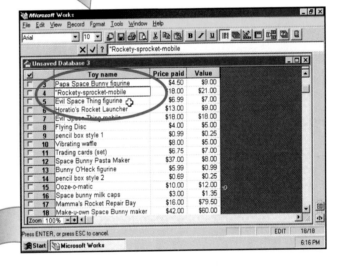

3 When you finish making changes, press **Enter**. Works displays the changed version, surrounded by the thick black line that indicates this cell is active. ■

WHY WORRY?

If you accidentally change the wrong thing, just pull down the Edit menu and select the Undo Entry command. The old version reappears!

Erasing a Record

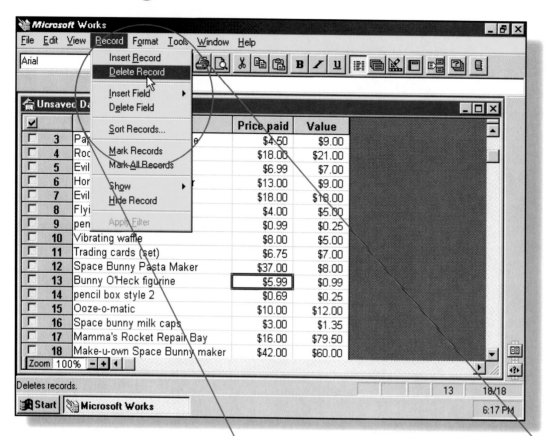

"Why would I do this?"

You can get rid of items you no longer want on your list. For example, if you had a database list of all of the things you planned to ask Santa Claus for, and someone gave you the solid mink cat warmer for your birthday in November, you could erase that item from your Christmas list database.

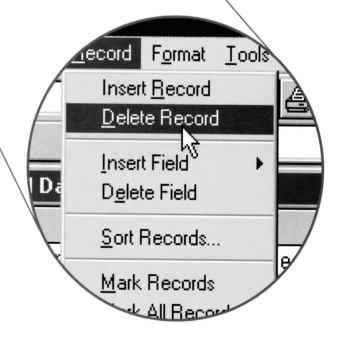

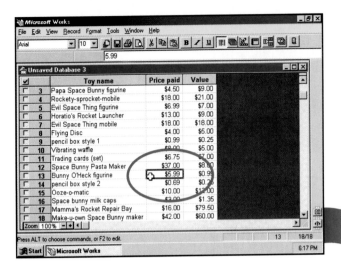

1 Click on any field in the record you want to delete.

NOTE ▼

When you create your database, think about whether you want to actually erase things from it, or whether you want to create a special field to place those old items in. Sometimes it's handy to keep a record of everything that was ever on your list.

2 Pull down the **Record** menu and select the **Delete Record** command.

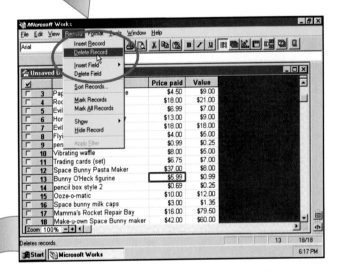

3 The selected record disappears, and all records after it move up one row to fill its space. ■

WHY WORRY?

If you accidentally delete the wrong record, pull down the Edit menu and select the Undo Delete Record command. The record reappears, right where it was!

191

TASK 60
Sorting Your Database

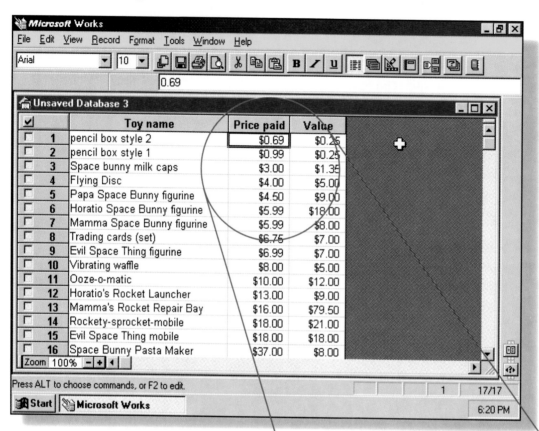

"Why would I do this?"

You can have Works sort your database and put the records in alphabetical or numerical order so you can quickly find what you are looking for. Works can arrange the records in order based on the information in any of the fields. You can sort the database again at any time to show the records in whatever order you want.

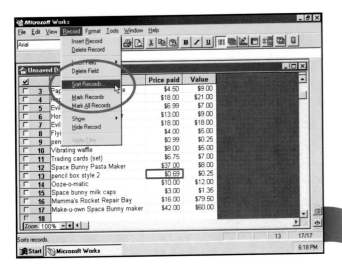

1 Pull down the **Record** menu and select the **Sort Records** command.

2 If Works displays this dialog box, click on the **OK** button to continue.

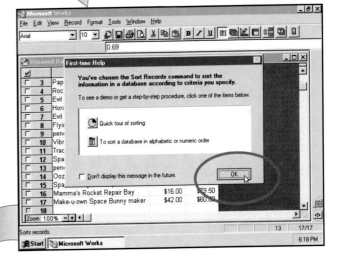

NOTE

To have Works show you some things about sorting, click on the button next to `Quick tour of sorting`. To skip over this screen in the future, click on the "Don't display this message in the future" check box at the bottom of the window.

3 In the Sort Records dialog box, click on the drop-down arrow under Sort by, and a list of fields appears.

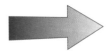

4 Click on the field that contains the information you want Works to use to put your records in order. If you choose a text field, Works puts the records in alphabetical order. If you choose a number field, Works puts them in order from lowest to highest. If you choose a date field, they will go in order from earliest date to latest date. Click on the `Descending` option button to reverse the order (Z through A, highest to lowest, or latest to earliest).

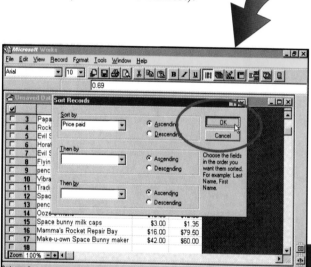

5 Click on the **OK** button.

NOTE ▼

If two records happen to have the same information in this field, you need to select another field to use as a tie-breaker. To do so, click on the drop-down arrow under Then by and repeat step 4.

6 Works sorts the records in the database and displays them in order. If you add records to your database at a later time, you have to sort again to get those records in the right place. ∎

WHY WORRY?

If you picked the wrong field to sort on, just sort it again!

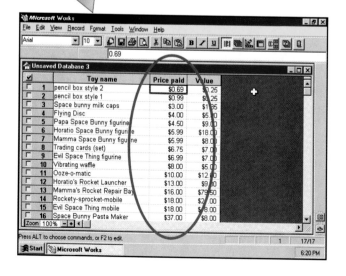

Using a Filter

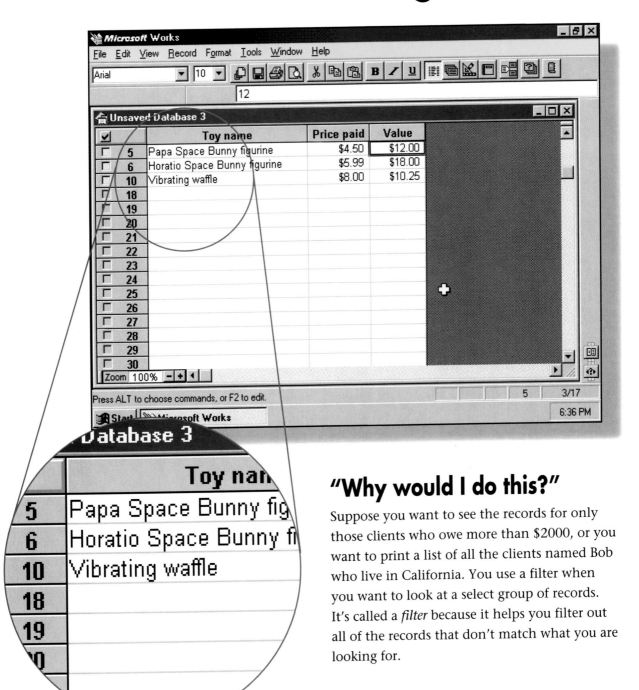

"Why would I do this?"

Suppose you want to see the records for only those clients who owe more than $2000, or you want to print a list of all the clients named Bob who live in California. You use a filter when you want to look at a select group of records. It's called a *filter* because it helps you filter out all of the records that don't match what you are looking for.

1 Click on the **Filters** button.

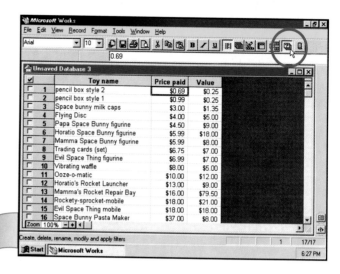

2 If Works displays this dialog box, click on the **OK** button to continue.

NOTE ▼

> To have Works show you some things about filters, click on the button next to Quick tour of filters. To skip over this screen in the future, click on the "Don't display this message in the future" check box at the bottom of the window.

3 The Filter dialog box appears. To reuse a filter that you've already made for this database, click on the drop-down arrow next to Filter name. A list of filter names appears. Click on the name of the filter you want to use, and then jump ahead to step 11.

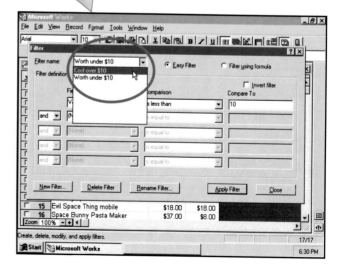

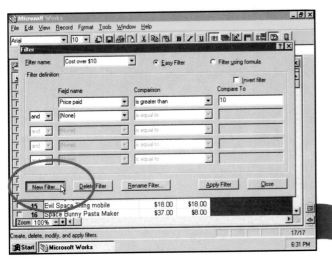

4 If you've already created a filter for this database but want to make another one, click on the **New Filter** button. If you have not created a filter for this database before, you don't have to do this because Works knows you want a new filter.

5 Works displays the Filter Name dialog box. Type in a name for your filter using up to fifteen letters and spaces.

> **NOTE** ▼
>
> Be sure to use a name you'll recognize later, in case you want to reuse this filter.

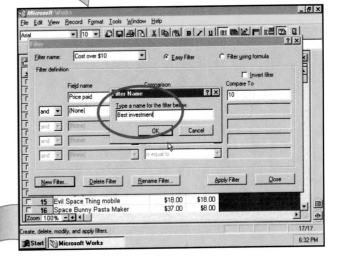

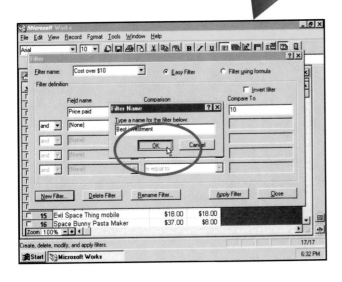

6 Click on the **OK** button. The Filter Name dialog box goes away.

7 Click on the drop-down arrow under Field name, and a list of field names appears. Click on the one you want Works to search and filter.

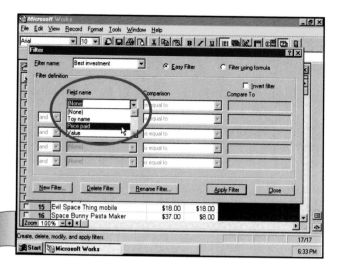

8 Click on the drop-down arrow under Comparison, and a list of phrases appears. Click on **is equal to** to see only those records where the data in the field is exactly the same as what you specify. If you're filtering a number field, you can click on **is less than** or **is greater than** to find numbers less or greater than a certain value.

NOTE ▼

For text fields, "less than" and "greater than" mean before and after in alphabetical order. For date fields, they mean before and after a given date.

9 In the Compare To text box, type the value you want Works to compare to the field's entries. For a number field, type a number. For a date field, type a date. For a text field, type whatever text you are looking for.

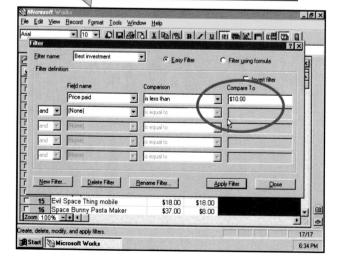

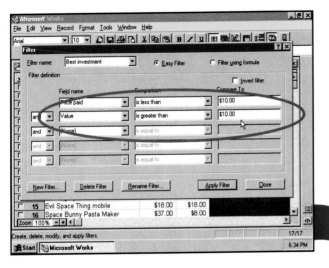

10 If you want to filter records based on more guidelines, repeat steps 7, 8, and 9 to fill in the second row of boxes. If you join them with "and," Works shows only the records that match both phrases. If you join them with "or," Works shows records that match either phrase.

NOTE ▼

You can filter by as many as five phrases at one time.

11 When you finish entering all the filter criteria, click on the **Apply Filter** button.

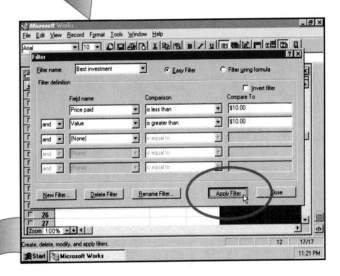

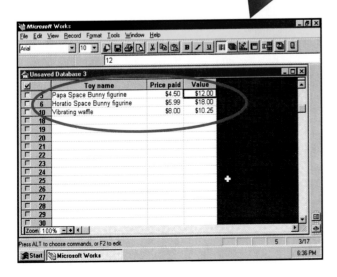

12 Works filters the database and displays only the records that make it through the filter. ∎

WHY WORRY?

To see all the records again, pull down the Record menu and select the Show command. A submenu appears off to the side. Select the All Records command, and all the records reappear!

TASK 62
Printing a List

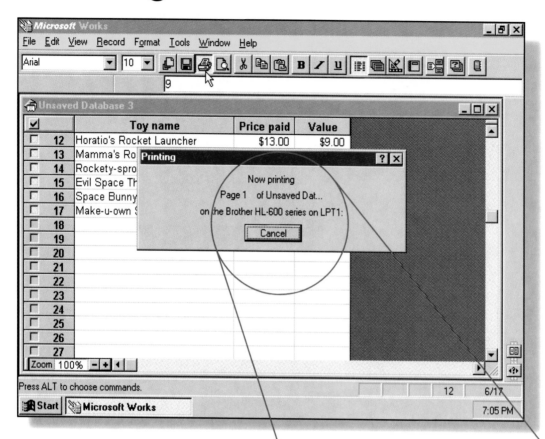

"Why would I do this?"

Once you print a list, you have your records on paper so you can carry them around, show them to people, or pass them on to others who might need the information. You can print out your entire database, or you can filter the list and then print only those selected parts of your database.

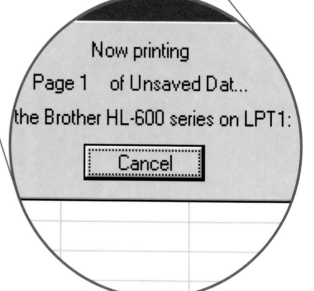

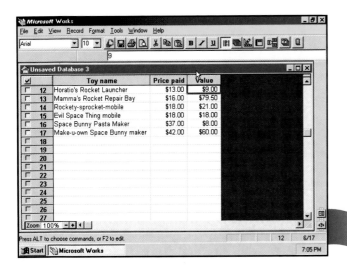

1 If you want your printed list to be sorted, sort it before you go any further. Then, if you want to print only selected parts of your list, start your filter.

NOTE ▼

Records wider than the screen will print across two pages. To avoid this, pull down the Edit menu and select the Select All command. Then pick a smaller type size from the Font Size box on the toolbar to shrink your fields so they all fit on one screen.

2 Click on the **Print** button.

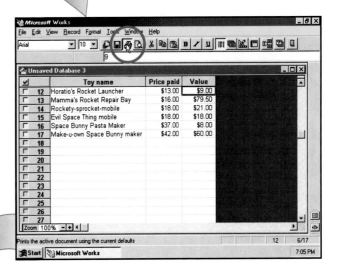

3 Works displays the Printing dialog box while it's sending the list to the printer. When the box disappears, you can continue working with your database. ■

WHY WORRY?

If you want to stop the printing job, just click on the Cancel button.

TASK 63

Leaving the Database Program

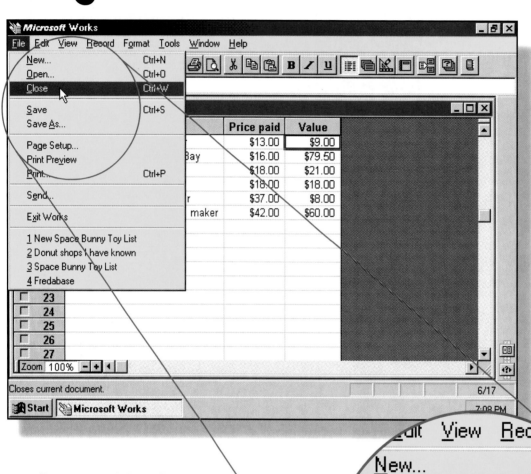

"Why would I do this?"

When you finish creating your database, making changes to it, or printing lists, you'll want to leave the database program so you can work on other things. But before you leave, you'll want to save any database changes on your hard disk, so the changes will still be there the next time you want to work with the database.

x

202

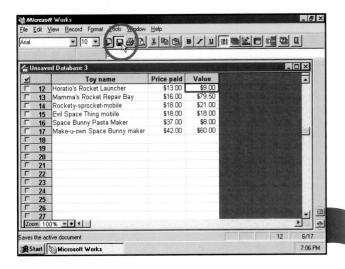

1 Click on the **Save** button. If you loaded this database from the disk or have previously saved it to the disk, Works replaces the copy already on the disk with this one. You can continue working with your file if you want.

2 If you have not saved this database before, you have to give it a name in the Save As dialog box. Be sure to use a name you can recognize, that is different from the name of any other database.

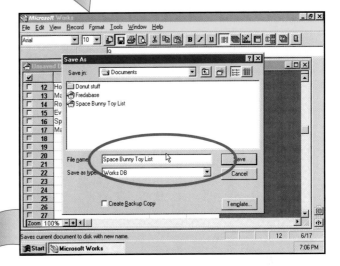

3 Click on the **Save** button, and Works saves the database on the disk.

WHY WORRY?

If you decide you don't want to save the file right now, click on the Cancel button. You can then continue working on your database.

4 If Works tells you The filename already exists, you have already used that name for another database. Click on the **No** button.

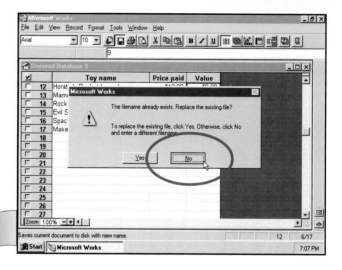

5 The Save As dialog box reappears. Type in a different name and click on the **Save** button. Once you have saved the database on disk, you can safely leave the program.

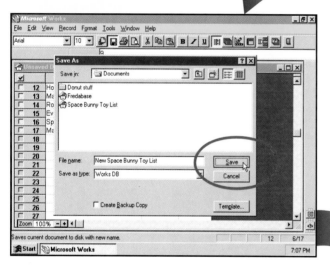

6 Pull down the **File** menu and select the **Close** command. Works closes the database program and returns you to the Task Launcher. ■

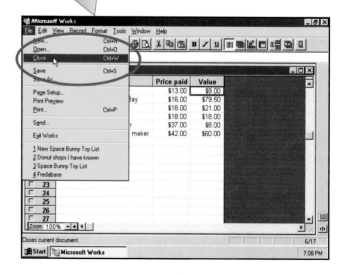

WHY WORRY?

If you leave the program and then realize you aren't finished working with your database, just load the database again and get back to work.

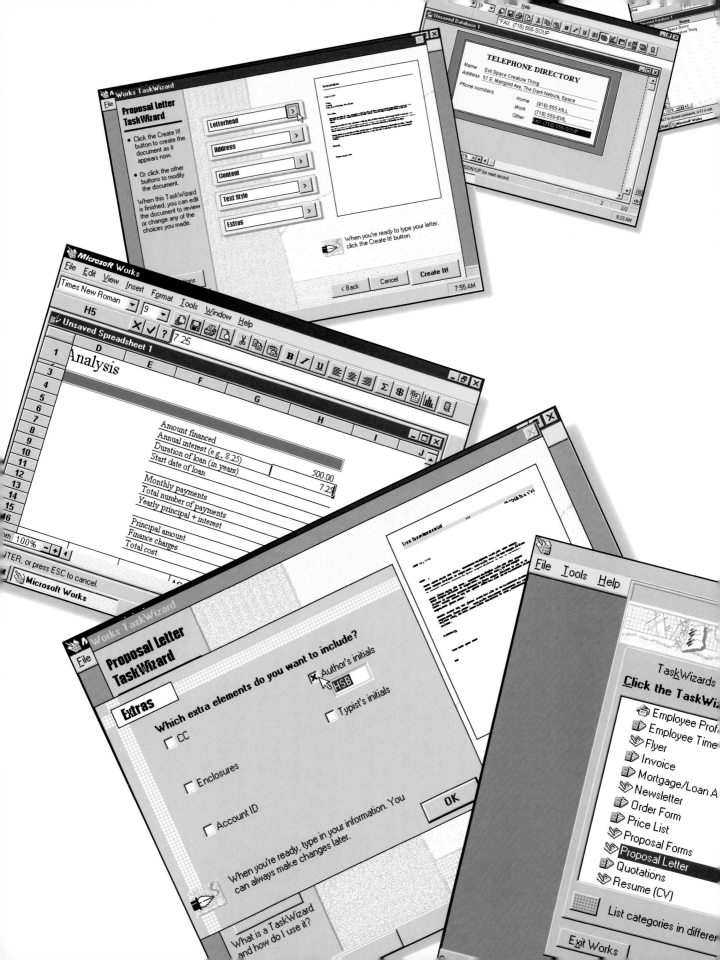

PART VI

Using a TaskWizard

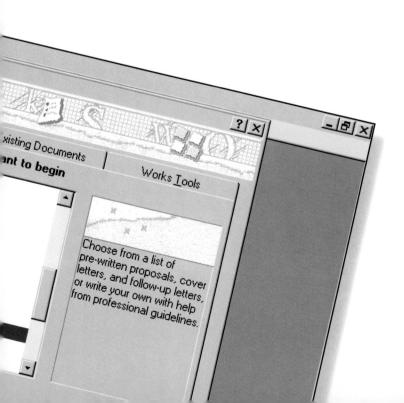

Choose from a list of pre-written proposals, cover letters, and follow-up letters, or write your own with help from professional guidelines.

ATaskWizard is a special tool in Works that enables you to do certain jobs quickly and easily. You can use a TaskWizard to create word processor documents, spreadsheets, and databases. Of course, you can also do each of these tasks on your own, but the TaskWizards save you time and effort.

Works provides two basic types of word processor TaskWizards. One type creates a sharply designed page with which you can make such things as fancy-looking newsletters or your own company letterhead. The other type provides you with your choice of completely prewritten letters, including everything from business proposal letters to thank-you notes. You can open a premade letter and make changes to it so that it will look like a letter you wrote.

The spreadsheet TaskWizards make spreadsheets for you with all the calculations set up and everything designed to look nice. Works includes premade spreadsheets designed to calculate loan payments, figure out your students' grades, and perform many other personal and business math calculations.

You can use the database TaskWizards to create a number of common databases. You don't have to worry about what fields to create or how wide to make them. All you have to do is enter the information, and the TaskWizards even provide an easy-to-use on-screen form for doing just that. These TaskWizards can create special databases for a range of uses including address books, CD collection lists, and employee information.

When you use a letter, spreadsheet, or database created by a TaskWizard, remember this: everything the TaskWizard makes, you can make too using normal Works commands. You, too, can create things like colored text, spreadsheets without the grid lines, and nice-looking forms for putting information into your database. You just need to learn some more advanced Works commands that aren't covered in this book. If you're interested in creating such effects, look carefully at what the TaskWizard has made and poke around the Help index a bit to find instructions for how to do it yourself when you aren't using the TaskWizard.

Essentially, TaskWizards help you in three ways. They enable you to do things that you already know how to do, faster than you could have done them by yourself. They enable you to do things that you don't already know how to do, without your having to learn them. And they point out to you things that you don't already know about Works.

The best way to learn more about TaskWizards and what they can do for you is to actually use a few of them. Follow the directions in this chapter, and don't be afraid to experiment—just to see what happens. Remember that you are creating *new* documents, spreadsheets, and databases, so nothing you do will mess up anything you've done before. And if you skip the step where you save what you've worked on, your experiment won't even take up space on your hard disk.

This is the last set of instructions in the book (although there are some sample documents and some handy reference items after it). When you're done with this section, you'll have a good working knowledge of Works. To commemorate this, start up the Certificate TaskWizard (it's in the set of Correspondence TaskWizards) and make yourself a certificate showing that you are now a trained Works user! If you've learned it, you've earned it—and there's no reason you shouldn't show it off!

Choosing a TaskWizard

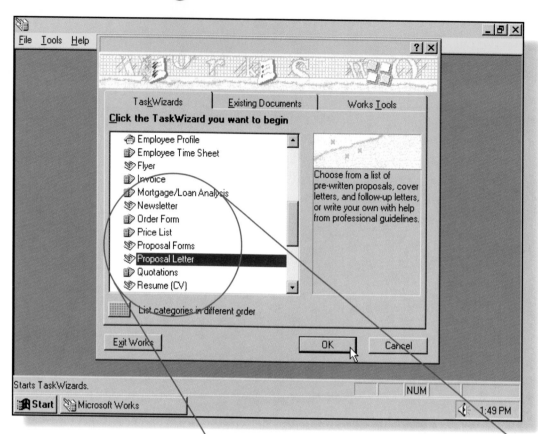

"Why Would I Do This?"

Because Works has dozens of TaskWizards to choose from, you have to choose a TaskWizard so Works knows what you want the TaskWizard to do.

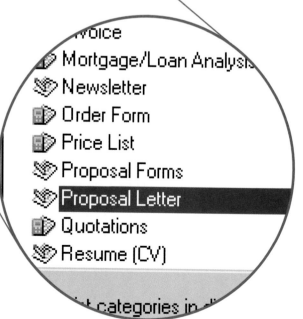

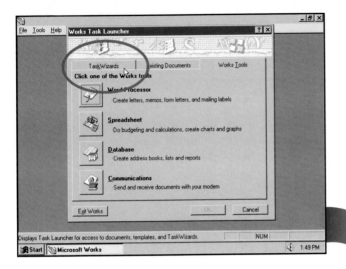

1 On the Task Launcher screen, click on the **TaskWizards** tab.

2 A list of TaskWizard categories appears. The categories themselves are shown in bold print; under some categories, you may see a list of TaskWizards in that category.

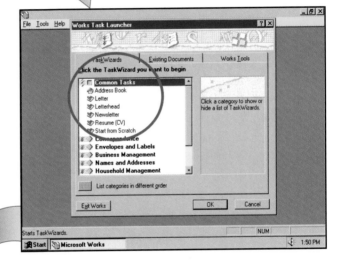

3 Scroll through the list to find the category that's most like what you want to do. If there is not a list of TaskWizards directly under it, click on the category name, and the list appears.

NOTE ▼

To get rid of a list of TaskWizards, just click on the category name.

4 Click on the name of the TaskWizard you want to run. The name becomes highlighted, and a description of what that TaskWizard creates appears on the right side of the window.

NOTE ▼

The little picture next to the TaskWizard name tells you what kind it is. A picture of a pencil and paper means it's a word processor TaskWizard. A calculator and a pad indicate it's a spreadsheet TaskWizard. Little Rolodex cards signify a database TaskWizard.

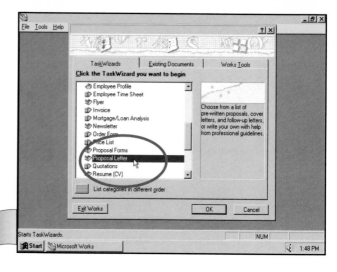

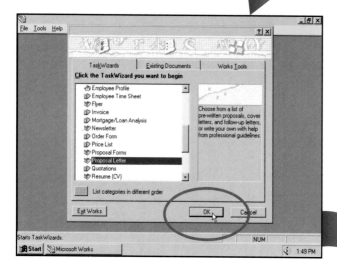

5 Click on the **OK** button.

WHY WORRY?

If you can't find a TaskWizard that seems to do what you want to do, click on the Works Tools tab and pick the appropriate program so you can do it yourself.

6 Works displays this dialog box to confirm that you want to use a TaskWizard. Click on the **Yes, run the TaskWizard** button. ■

WHY WORRY?

If you change your mind about running the TaskWizard now, just click on the Cancel button to get back to the Task Launcher.

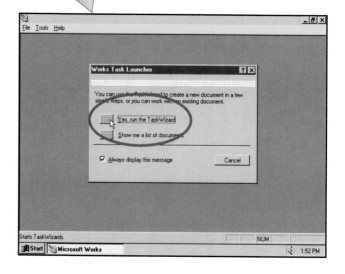

Choosing Your Options

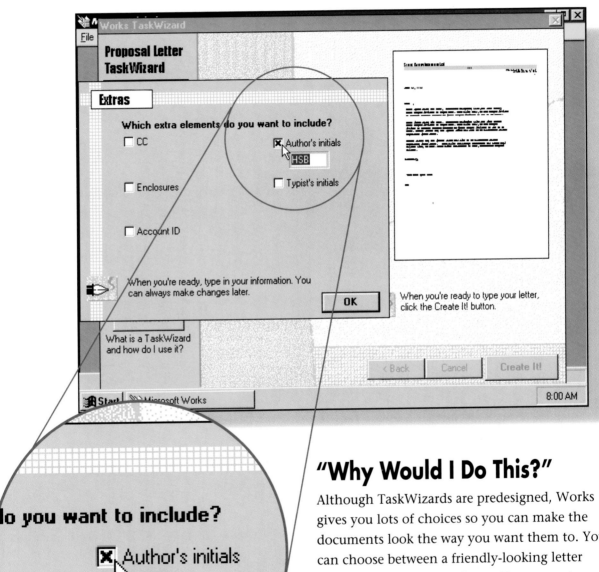

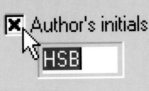

"Why Would I Do This?"

Although TaskWizards are predesigned, Works gives you lots of choices so you can make the documents look the way you want them to. You can choose between a friendly-looking letter and a down-to-business letter. You can put your name and address in a letter, and you can make a spreadsheet show more- or less-detailed information. Every TaskWizard gives you some choices about the document you're creating, but what those choices are depends on the document.

213

1 Works presents you with several basic designs for your document. Each one has either a small picture of the document or a picture that indicates what it's used for, with a short description under it.

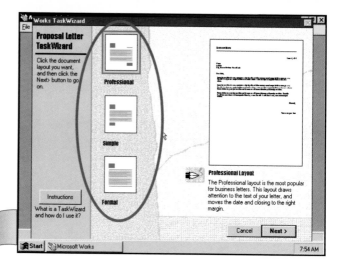

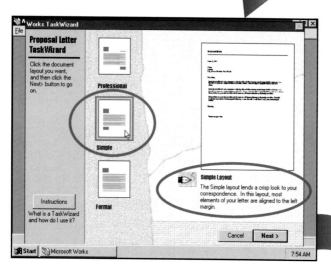

2 Click on the picture for the design you like. A rectangle appears around the picture to show it's selected, and Works displays a short description of that design on the right side of the screen.

> **NOTE** ▼
>
> If you can tell from the description that you don't want this design, just click on another picture and see what that design is like.

3 Look in the lower-right corner of the box. If you see a button labeled Create it!, you've selected all the options, and you're finished with this task. If not, click on the **Next >** button.

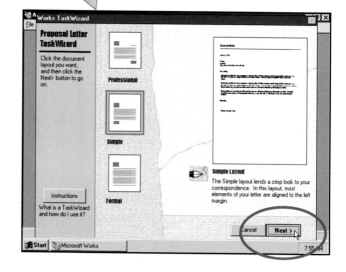

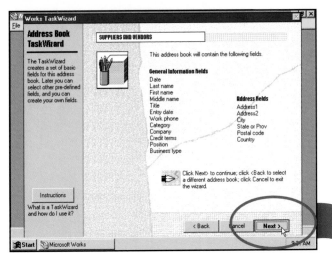

4 Works displays another screen of information. Read the information and, if this screen has a Next > button, click on it.

5 The next screen should show a small picture of your document on the right. In the middle of the screen, you see some options with > buttons next to them. Click on the first > button, and a box with that set of options appears.

NOTE ▼

When you click on some of these options, a box appears in which you must type information related to that option (such as your name if you checked an option that tells the TaskWizard to put your name in the document).

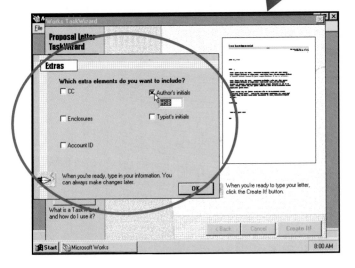

6 If the options have small squares (called *check boxes*) next to them, you can select as many of the options as you want. Click on the check box next to the options you want. When an option is selected (turned on), an X appears in its square. (You can click again to remove the X and turn off the option.)

7 If the options have small circles (called *option buttons*) next to them, you can only pick one. Click on the circle for the option you want, and a dot appears in the circle to show it's selected.

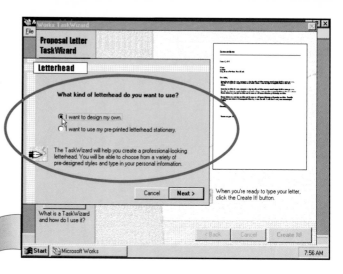

WHY WORRY?

If you click on the wrong circle, just click again on the right one. When you do, the dot disappears from the circle that was selected and appears in the newly selected circle.

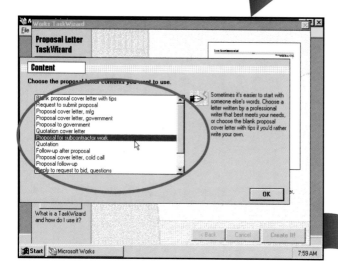

8 Depending on the option you selected, the TaskWizard might present you with a list of possibilities. Click on the one you want.

NOTE ▼

Works remembers what you typed in the last time it asked for this information and displays that in the boxes. If the correct information is already there, you don't have to retype it.

9 If the TaskWizard presents you with a screen like this, Works is looking for information. Click on each white rectangle (called a *text box*) in turn, and the blinking cursor appears there. Then type in the appropriate information. (You can leave some blank, if you want.)

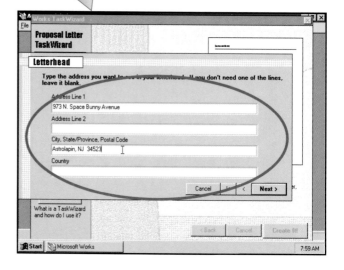

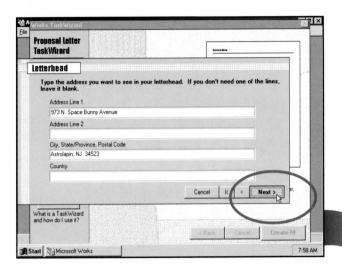

10 When you finish choosing options, click on the button in the lower-right corner of the box. If it's an OK button, you are done with that set of options. If it's a Next > button, you'll see another box of options in that set.

11 Repeat steps 5 through 10 for each of the sets of options.

WHY WORRY?

If you make a mistake when choosing options, just reselect the option and change it. If you mistakenly chose the wrong design, hit the Back button to go back to the screen where you can choose a different design.

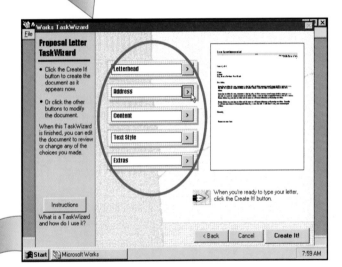

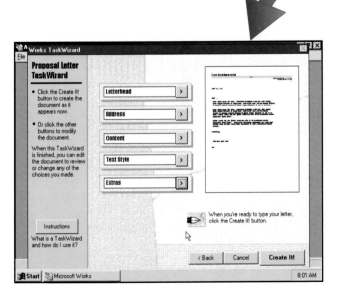

12 When you finish selecting all of your options, you're ready to have the TaskWizard actually make your document. ∎

TASK 66

Creating the Final Product

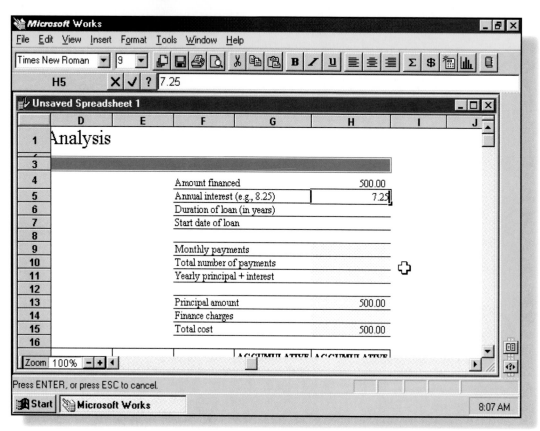

"Why Would I Do This?"

Once you've given the TaskWizard all the information, it's time to let the TaskWizard do its job. You tell the TaskWizard to create the spreadsheet, database, or word processor document, and then you use Works to take advantage of the result.

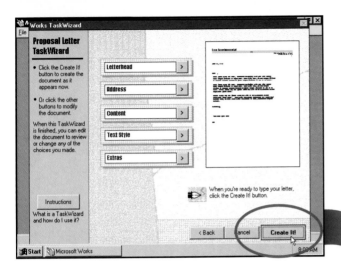

1 Click on the **Create It!** button. This tells the TaskWizard to take all the information you've given it and actually build a document.

2 Some TaskWizards display another screen, which has a Create Document button in the lower-right corner. If this screen appears, click on the **Create Document** button.

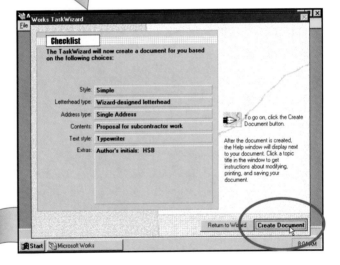

3 Works displays this dialog box while it sets up the document to your specifications. When the TaskWizard finishes creating the document, the box disappears, and you see the program for the type of document you requested.

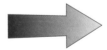

219

4 If you used a word processor TaskWizard, you're now in the word processor, and the document that the TaskWizard created is open. You can work with it as you would with any other word processor document.

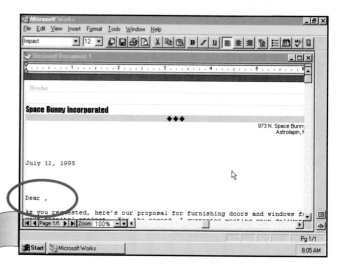

5 Be sure to read through the entire document. The TaskWizard cannot always customize everything; sometimes it gives you generic information that you can use with a little cutting and pasting.

NOTE ▼

These documents often include a list of suggestions about how to change them for most effective use. Read these suggestions and then delete them.

6 If the TaskWizard made a spreadsheet, you're going to have to fill in the data for the calculations. The cells are labeled, so you can tell what goes where. Don't type in cells that contain gray dots; gray dots indicate that the cell will contain the answer to a calculation.

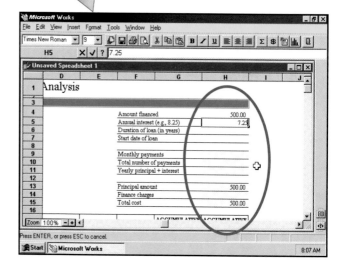

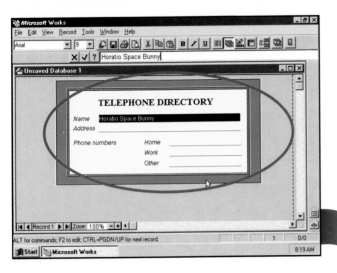

7 If the TaskWizard has made a database, you see a form to put your information into (instead of just a grid). The blanks for each field are marked so that you can tell what information goes in that field. Type the information for the first field.

8 When you're done with that field, press **Tab** to move to the next field. When you've filled in the last field for the record, press **Tab** again, and Works displays a blank form for the next entry.

> **NOTE** ▼
>
> You can also hold down the Ctrl key and press PgUp to move back, or hold the Ctrl key and press PgDn to move forward.

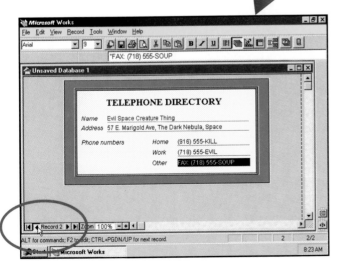

9 You can flip through the records using the buttons to the left and right of the record number display. Click on the left arrow button to move back one record; click on the right arrow button to move forward one record.

221

10 If you prefer to work with the grid instead of the forms, click on the **List View** button to see the database as a grid. (Some databases that the TaskWizard creates don't look right in this view because they don't show all of the fields.)

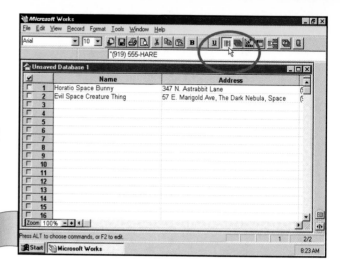

11 To go back to the database's form, just click on the **Form View** button.

WHY WORRY?

If you don't like what the TaskWizard made for you, pull down the File menu and select the Close command. When Works asks you if you want to save what you've worked on, click the No button. Then try the TaskWizard again with different options, or try making it yourself from scratch.

12 Whether you made a word processor document, a spreadsheet, or a database, remember to save it before you leave the program. When you save it, you have to give it a name; the TaskWizard does not automatically name things. ■

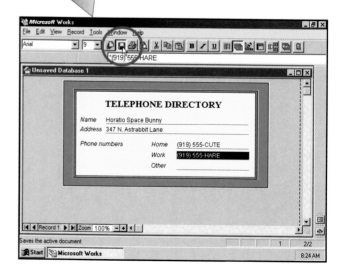

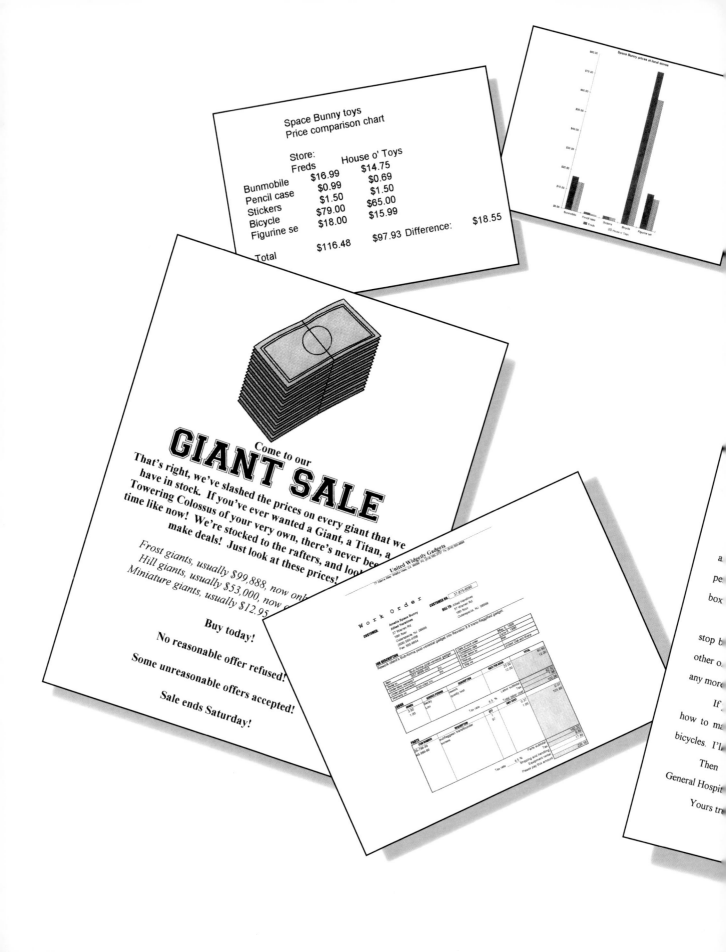

Space Bunny toys
Price comparison chart

	Store: Freds	House o' Toys
Bunmobile	$16.99	$14.75
Pencil case	$0.99	$0.69
Stickers	$1.50	$1.50
Bicycle	$79.00	$65.00
Figurine se	$18.00	$15.99
Total	$116.48	$97.93 Difference: $18.55

Space Bunny prices at local stores

Come to our
GIANT SALE
That's right, we've slashed the prices on every giant that we have in stock. If you've ever wanted a Giant, a Titan, a Towering Colossus of your very own, there's never been a time like now! We're stocked to the rafters, and look... make deals! Just look at these prices!

Frost giants, usually $99,888, now onl...
Hill giants, usually $53,000, now ...
Miniature giants, usually $12.95...

Buy today!

No reasonable offer refused!

Some unreasonable offers accepted!

Sale ends Saturday!

United Widgetly Gadgets

Work Order

CUSTOMER NO. 37-878-6090

PART VII

Sample Documents

▼ Create a Simple Letter

▼ Create an Advertising Flyer

▼ Create a Spreadsheet and Graph

▼ Create a Work Order

▼ Create a Phone Number and Birthday List

Space Bunny,   January 15th, 1996

you're the cutest! The absolutely cutest thing in the whole world! I have
es on video tape, plus all your toys except for the Horatio Space Bunny
2, which I used to have but my sister stole. So I took her favorite lunch
the dumpster. That'll show her!
as wondering if you would ever come to visit Earth. If you do, please
I live in the big green house. Not the one with the elm tree, the
at used to have a penguin statue in the front yard, only it isn't there

an have a good time. We can eat candy carrots if you'll show me
we can watch all your movies, and we can ride around on
if you don't have a bicycle.
here I work. I'm the Director of Podiatry at the Atterday
big white building with the helicopter landing place on top.

Moving text toward the right edge, page 63

Typing, page 39

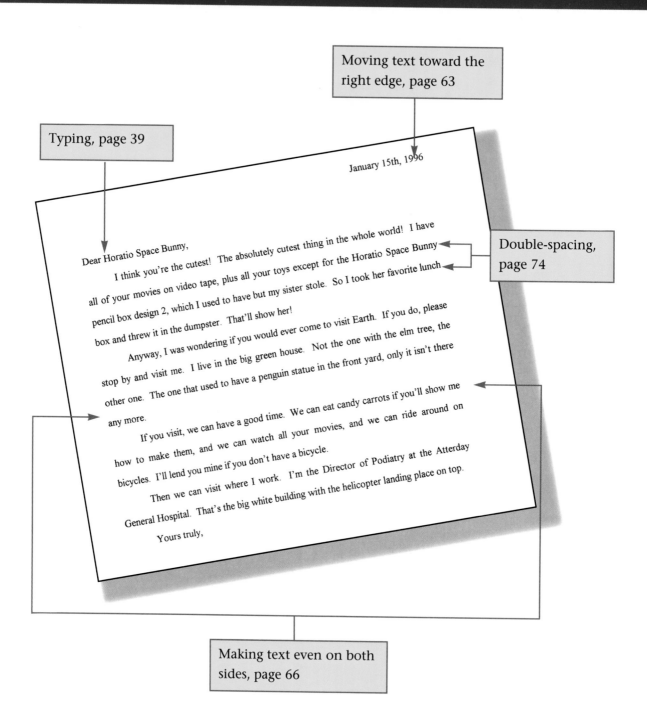

January 15th, 1996

Dear Horatio Space Bunny,

I think you're the cutest! The absolutely cutest thing in the whole world! I have all of your movies on video tape, plus all your toys except for the Horatio Space Bunny pencil box design 2, which I used to have but my sister stole. So I took her favorite lunch box and threw it in the dumpster. That'll show her!

Anyway, I was wondering if you would ever come to visit Earth. If you do, please stop by and visit me. I live in the big green house. Not the one with the elm tree, the other one. The one that used to have a penguin statue in the front yard, only it isn't there any more.

If you visit, we can have a good time. We can eat candy carrots if you'll show me how to make them, and we can watch all your movies, and we can ride around on bicycles. I'll lend you mine if you don't have a bicycle.

Then we can visit where I work. I'm the Director of Podiatry at the Atterday General Hospital. That's the big white building with the helicopter landing place on top.

Yours truly,

Double-spacing, page 74

Making text even on both sides, page 66

Create a Simple Letter

1 Start up the word processing program with a new, blank document. See these tasks for help on this step:

Starting Works	*TASK 2, p. 12*
Starting a New Document	*TASK 9, p. 34*

2 Type in the letter. The following task tells you how to type a document and make simple corrections:

Typing	*TASK 11, p. 39*

3 Select the date and move it to the right of the page. See these tasks:

Selecting Text	*TASK 14, p. 47*
Moving Text Toward the Center or the Right Edge	*TASK 20, p. 63*

4 Select the main body of the letter, put a blank line between the lines of text, and make the right edge smooth. These tasks show you how to do this:

Selecting Text	*TASK 14, p. 47*
Double-Spacing	*TASK 24, p. 74*
Making Text Even on Both Sides	*TASK 21, p. 66*

5 Print the letter out and save it on disk. See these tasks for printing and saving:

Printing Your Document	*TASK 28, p. 89*
Saving Your Document	*TASK 29, p. 91*

Adding a picture, page 77

Changing the font, page 60

Come to our
GIANT SALE

That's right, we've slashed the prices on every giant that we have in stock. If you've ever wanted a Giant, a Titan, a Towering Colossus of your very own, there's never been a time like now! We're stocked to the rafters, and looking to make deals! Just look at these prices!

Frost giants, usually $99,888, now only $75,000!
Hill giants, usually $53,000, now only $47,000!
Miniature giants, usually $12.95, now two for $20!

Buy today!

No reasonable offer refused!

Some unreasonable offers accepted!

Sale ends Saturday!

Making text bold or italic, page 58

Moving text toward the center, page 63

Create an Advertising Flyer

1 Start up the word processing program with a new, blank document. See these tasks for help on this step:

Starting Works	*TASK 2, p. 12*
Starting a New Document	*TASK 9, p. 34*

2 Place a picture at the top. See the following task for instructions:

Adding a Picture	*TASK 25, p. 77*

3 Type in the text. This task tells you how to type a document and make simple corrections:

Typing	*TASK 11, p. 39*

4 Make some of the text larger, some thicker, some italic, and some a different type style. These tasks show you how to change the look of your text:

Selecting Text	*TASK 14, p. 47*
Making Text Bold, Italic, or Underlined	*TASK 18, p. 58*
Changing the Font	*TASK 19, p. 60*

5 Center all the text on the page. These tasks tell you how to do that:

Selecting Text	*TASK 14, p. 47*
Moving Text Toward the Center or the Right Edge	*TASK 20, p. 63*

6 Print the letter out and save it on disk. See these tasks for printing and saving instructions:

Printing Your Document	*TASK 28, p. 89*
Saving Your Document	*TASK 29, p. 91*

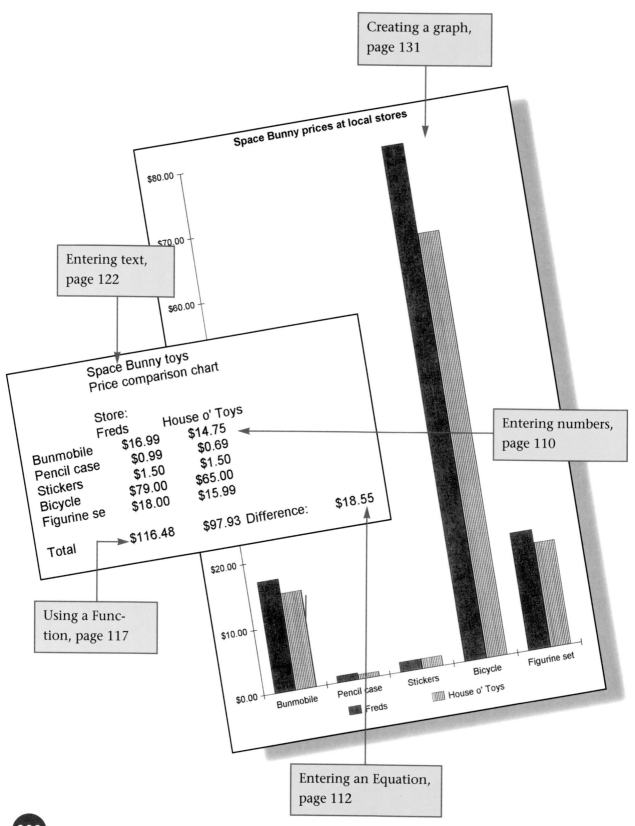

Creating a graph, page 131

Space Bunny prices at local stores

Entering text, page 122

$80.00

$70.00

$60.00

Space Bunny toys
Price comparison chart

Store:
Freds   House o' Toys
$14.75
Bunmobile $16.99 $0.69
Pencil case $0.99 $1.50
Stickers $1.50 $65.00
Bicycle $79.00 $15.99
Figurine se $18.00

$97.93 Difference: $18.55
Total $116.48

Entering numbers, page 110

Using a Func-
tion, page 117

$20.00

$10.00

$0.00   Bunmobile   Pencil case   Stickers   Bicycle   Figurine set

House o' Toys
Freds

Entering an Equation,
page 112

Create a Spreadsheet and Graph

1 Start up a new, blank spreadsheet. See these tasks for help on this step:

Starting Works   TASK 2, p. 12

Creating a New, Blank Spreadsheet   TASK 31, p. 100

2 Put all the text and the known numbers into the spreadsheet. These two tasks tell you how to do that:

Entering Text   TASK 38, p. 122

Entering Numbers   TASK 35, p. 110

3 Calculate the totals for each store and the difference between the totals. You learn about performing mathematical calculations in these tasks:

Entering an Equation   TASK 36, p. 112

Using a Function   TASK 37, p. 117

4 Display all the numbers as dollars and cents. Follow these tasks to do that:

Selecting a Range of Cells   TASK 34, p. 108

Showing Dollars and Cents   TASK 41, p. 129

5 Design and print the graph. Everything you need to know to create a graph is in this task:

Creating a Graph   TASK 42, p. 131

6 Print the spreadsheet and save it on disk using the steps in these tasks:

Printing Your Spreadsheet   TASK 43, p. 136

Saving Your Spreadsheet   TASK 44, p. 138

Starting up a
TaskWizard, page 210

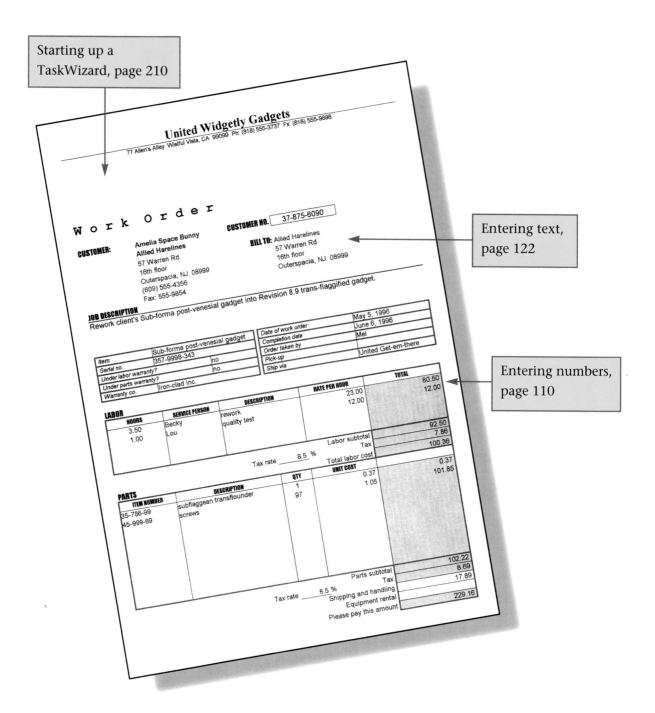

United Widgetly Gadgets
77 Allen's Alley Wistful Vista, CA 99099 Ph: (818) 555-3737 Fx: (818) 555-9898

W o r k   O r d e r

CUSTOMER NO. | 37-875-6090

CUSTOMER: Amelia Space Bunny
Allied Harelines
57 Warren Rd
16th floor
Outerspacia, NJ 08999
(609) 555-4356
Fax: 555-9854

BILL TO: Allied Harelines
57 Warren Rd
16th floor
Outerspacia, NJ 08999

Entering text,
page 122

JOB DESCRIPTION
Rework client's Sub-forma post-venesial gadget into Revision 8.9 trans-flaggified gadget.

				Date of work order	May 5, 1996		
	Sub-forma post-venesial gadget			Completion date	June 6, 1996		
Item	357-9998-343	no		Order taken by	Mel		
Serial no.		no		Pick-up			
Under labor warranty?				Ship via	United Get-em-there		
Under parts warranty?							
Warranty co.	Iron-clad Inc.					**TOTAL**	

LABOR				**RATE PER HOUR**			80.50
HOURS	**SERVICE PERSON**	**DESCRIPTION**		23.00			12.00
3.50	Becky	rework		12.00			
1.00	Lou	quality test					92.50
				Labor subtotal			7.86
				Tax			100.36
	Tax rate	8.5 %		Total labor cost			

Entering numbers,
page 110

PARTS			**QTY**	**UNIT COST**			0.37
ITEM NUMBER	**DESCRIPTION**		1	0.37			101.85
35-786-99	subflaggean transflounder		97	1.05			
45-999-89	screws						
							102.22
				Parts subtotal			8.69
				Tax			17.89
	Tax rate	8.5 %		Shipping and handling			
				Equipment rental			229.16
				Please pay this amount			

Create a Work Order

1 Use the Work Order TaskWizard. The tasks involved in this are:

Starting Works	*TASK 2, p. 12*
Starting Up a TaskWizard	*TASK 64, p. 210*
Setting Your Options	*TASK 65, p. 213*
Creating the Final Product	*TASK 66, p. 218*

2 Fill in the blanks on the work order. There are two tasks for doing this, one for filling in numbers, the other for filling in words:

Entering Numbers	*TASK 35, p. 110*
Entering Text	*TASK 38, p. 122*

3 Print the spreadsheet and save it on disk using the steps in these tasks:

Printing Your Spreadsheet	*TASK 43, p. 136*
Saving Your Spreadsheet	*TASK 44, p. 138*

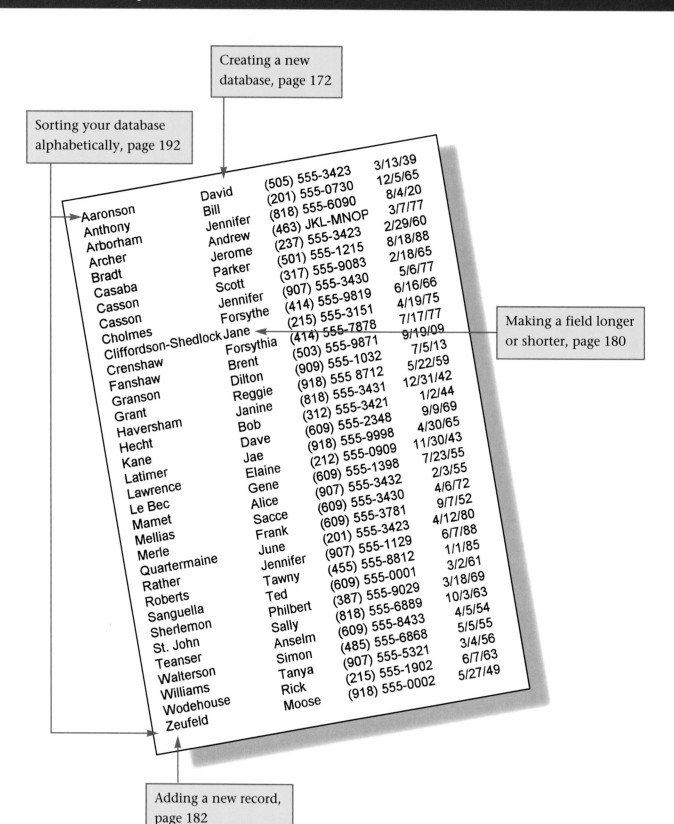

Creating a new
database, page 172

Sorting your database
alphabetically, page 192

	David	(505) 555-3423	3/13/39
	Bill	(201) 555-0730	12/5/65
Aaronson	Jennifer	(818) 555-6090	8/4/20
Anthony	Andrew	(463) JKL-MNOP	3/7/77
Arborham	Jerome	(237) 555-3423	2/29/60
Archer	Parker	(501) 555-1215	8/18/88
Bradt	Scott	(317) 555-9083	2/18/65
Casaba	Jennifer	(907) 555-3430	5/6/77
Casson	Forsythe	(414) 555-9819	6/16/66
Casson	Jane	(215) 555-3151	4/19/75
Cholmes		(414) 555-7878	7/17/77
Cliffordson-Shedlock	Forsythia	(503) 555-9871	9/19/09
Crenshaw	Brent	(909) 555-1032	7/5/13
Fanshaw	Dilton	(918) 555 8712	5/22/59
Granson	Reggie	(818) 555-3431	12/31/42
Grant	Janine	(312) 555-3421	1/2/44
Haversham	Bob	(609) 555-2348	9/9/69
Hecht	Dave	(918) 555-9998	4/30/65
Kane	Jae	(212) 555-0909	11/30/43
Latimer	Elaine	(609) 555-1398	7/23/55
Lawrence	Gene	(907) 555-3432	2/3/55
Le Bec	Alice	(609) 555-3430	4/6/72
Mamet	Sacce	(609) 555-3781	9/7/52
Mellias	Frank	(201) 555-3423	4/12/80
Merle	June	(907) 555-1129	6/7/88
Quartermaine	Jennifer	(455) 555-8812	1/1/85
Rather	Tawny	(609) 555-0001	3/2/61
Roberts	Ted	(387) 555-9029	3/18/69
Sanguella	Philbert	(818) 555-6889	10/3/63
Sherlemon	Sally	(609) 555-8433	4/5/54
St. John	Anselm	(485) 555-6868	5/5/55
Teanser	Simon	(907) 555-5321	3/4/56
Walterson	Tanya	(215) 555-1902	6/7/63
Williams	Rick	(918) 555-0002	5/27/49
Wodehouse	Moose		
Zeufeld			

Making a field longer
or shorter, page 180

Adding a new record,
page 182

Create a Phone Number and Birthday List

1 Create a new database with fields for last name, first name, phone number, and birthday. The tasks for doing this are:

Starting Works	TASK 2, p. 12
Creating a New Database	TASK 53, p. 172

2 Fill in the names, phone numbers, and birthdays by following the instructions in this task:

Adding a New Record	TASK 56, p. 182

3 Change the size of the fields to fit the data. The following task tells you how to do that:

Making a Field Longer or Shorter	TASK 55, p. 180

4 Arrange the list items in alphabetical order based on last name. See this task if you need help:

Sorting Your Database	TASK 60, p. 192

5 Print the list, save it on your disk, and leave the database program. Those skills are covered in these two tasks:

Printing a List	TASK 62, p. 200
Leaving the Database	TASK 63, p. 202

PART VIII

Reference

▼ Quick Reference

▼ Toolbar Guide

Quick Reference

Use these tables when you need a reminder of how to use the features of each Works program. For each feature, we've included the menu name, the command for the feature, and its shortcut key (if there is one). The "Ctrl+" key combination indicates that you must hold down the Ctrl key and press whichever key is listed after the plus. For more information on a particular feature, check out its related tasks.

Word Processor Reference

Feature	Menu	Command	Shortcut Key
Align text	Format	Font and Style	(none)
Bold text	Format	Font and Style	Ctrl+B
Copy text	Edit	Copy	Ctrl+C and then
	Edit	Paste	Ctrl+V
Erase text	Edit	Cut	Ctrl+X
Find a word	Edit	Find	Ctrl+F
Help	Help	Contents	F1
Italic text	Format	Font and Style	Ctrl+I
Justified text	Format	Paragraph	(none)
Leave document	File	Close	Ctrl+W
Line Spacing	Format	Paragraph	(none)
Margins	File	Page Setup	(none)
New page	Insert	Page Break	Ctrl+Enter
Picture	Insert	ClipArt	(none)
Print	File	Print	Ctrl+P
Save document	File	Save	Ctrl+S
Select everything	Edit	Select All	Ctrl+A
Spelling check	Tools	Spelling	F7
Type style	Format	Font and Style	(none)
Underlined text	Format	Font and Style	Ctrl+U
Zooming	View	Zoom	(none)

Spreadsheet Reference

Feature	Menu	Command	Shortcut Key
Copy cells	Edit	Copy	Ctrl+C
Paste cells	Edit	Paste	Ctrl+V
Erase cells	Edit	Cut	Ctrl+X
Go to a cell	Edit	Go To	F5 or Ctrl+G
Help	Help	Contents	F1
Leave spreadsheet	File	Close	Ctrl+W
Print	File	Print	Ctrl+P
Save spreadsheet	File	Save	Ctrl+S
Select everything	Edit	Select All	Ctrl+A
Show dollars and cents	Format	Number	Ctrl+4
Zoom	View	Zoom	(none)

Communications Reference

Feature	Menu	Command	Shortcut Key
Dial	Phone	Easy Connect	(none)
Hang up	Phone	Hangup	(none)
Help	Help	Contents	F1
Leave communications	File	Close	Ctrl+W

Database Reference

Feature	Menu	Command	Shortcut Key
Erase a record	Edit	Cut	Ctrl+X
Field Width	Format	Field Width	(none)
Filter	Tools	Filters	(none)
Find a record	Edit	Find	Ctrl+F
Go to last record		(none)	Ctrl+End
Help	Help	Contents	F1
Leaving database	File	Close	Ctrl+W
Print	File	Print	Ctrl+P
Saving database	File	Save	Ctrl+S
Selecting a record	Edit	Select Record	(none)
Selecting a field	Edit	Select Field	(none)
Sort database	Record	Sort Records	(none)

Toolbar Guide

A toolbar appears near the top of each program's screen. You can simply click on a Works toolbar button to bypass the menu system and perform the most common procedures quickly. The following tables show you the toolbar buttons available in each of the Works programs.

Word Processor Toolbar

Button	Name	Description
Times New Roman	Font name	Displays a list of available type styles
12	Font size	Displays a list of available type sizes
	Task Launcher	Opens the Task Launcher
	Save	Saves the document on disk
	Print	Prints the document
	Print Preview	Shows how document will look when printed
	Cut	Stores selected text in memory and then removes it from document
	Copy	Stores the selected text in memory
	Paste	Inserts the last text cut or copied
B	Bold	Makes text bold
I	Italic	Makes text italic
U	Underline	Underlines text
	Left Align	Lines up text at the left of the page
	Center Align	Lines up text at the center of the page
	Right Align	Lines up text at the right of the page
	Easy Formats	Helps you design your document
	Bullets	Adds dots in front of the elements in a list
	Lookup Reference	Starts other reference programs
	Spelling Checker	Checks for spelling mistakes
	Address Book	Displays your address database

Spreadsheet Toolbar

Button	Name	Description
Arial	Font name	Displays a list of available type styles
10	Font size	Displays a list of available type sizes
	Task Launcher	Opens the Task Launcher
	Save	Saves the spreadsheet on the disk
	Print	Prints the spreadsheet
	Print Preview	Shows how spreadsheet will look when printed
	Cut	Stores selected cells in memory and then removes them from the spreadsheet
	Copy	Stores the selected cells in memory
	Paste	Inserts the last cells cut or copied
B	Bold	Makes text bold
I	Italic	Makes text italic
U	Underline	Underlines the text
	Left Align	Starts text at the left edge of the cell
	Center Align	Centers text in the cell
	Right Align	Ends text at the right edge of the cell
Σ	AutoSum	Adds up figures
$	Currency	Shows numbers as dollars and cents
	Easy Calc	Helps you use formulas
	New Chart	Makes a graph
	Address Book	Displays your address database

Communications Toolbar

Button	Name	Description
	Task Launcher	Opens the Task Launcher
	Save	Saves settings on the disk
	Copy	Stores the screen text in memory
	Paste	Inserts the last text cut or copied
	Communications Settings	Changes modem information
	Terminal Settings	Changes terminal emulation
	Phone Settings	Changes redialing information
	Transfer Settings	Changes file exchange settings
	8-N-1 Settings	Uses the most common modem language
	7-E-1 Settings	Uses another common modem language
	Easy Connect	Lets you pick number to dial
	Dial/Hangup	Hangs up or redials phone
	Pause	Stops the current communications
	Capture Text	Puts arriving text in file
	Send Text	Sends text from file
	Send Binary File	Copies a file to another computer
	Receive Binary File	Copies a file from another computer
	Address Book	Displays your address database

Database Toolbar

Button	Name	Description
Arial	Font name	Displays a list of available type styles
10	Font size	Displays a list of available type sizes
	Task Launcher	Opens the Task Launcher
	Save	Saves the database on disk
	Print	Prints the database
	Print Preview	Shows how database will look when printed
	Cut	Stores selected fields or records in memory and then deletes them from the database
	Copy	Stores selected fields in memory
	Paste	Inserts the last fields cut or copied
B	Bold	Makes text bold
I	Italic	Makes text italic
U	Underline	Underlines the text
	List View	Shows records as list
	Form View	Shows records in a custom form
	Form Design	Lets you design a custom form
	Report View	Shows records with header and totals
	Insert Record	Opens up a new record space
	Filters	Lets you pick and design filters
	Address Book	Displays your address database

Index